BHU

GW00320484

APA PUBLICATIONS **L**

Part of the Langenscheidt Publishing Group

Paro Valley

4 km / 2.5 miles

Welcome!

Bhutan is a land of forests and fortresses, monasteries and mountains, a place where hardy people sing while they work and monks perform centuries-old rituals. With its remarkably well-preserved heritage, tradition in Bhutan is not a relic of the past, but a living and breathing element of daily life.

Guiding you to this little-known Himalayan kingdom is Insight's correspondent to Bhutan, Francoise Pommaret. With carefully-crafted itineraries that divide the country into four regions – Paro and Thimphu, Punakha and Wangdiphodrang, Central Bhutan, and East Bhutan – this book covers all of the country's major attractions, plus some of the lesser-known sights. Chapters on trekking, eating out and shopping, and a useful practical information section complete the Bhutan experience. This book is especially useful for the small number of visitors who are allowed to enter the country each year on packaged tours, both as a reference for pre-trip planning and for making suggestions to local tour guides while on the road.

 Francoise Pommaret, a French academic, travel guide and author of several books on Bhutan, first set eyes on the country in 1979, after an arduous journey through mountains and forests. Certain that hers was a quest to learn about the people and their culture, Pommaret stayed on, living and working for the Bhutanese government for several years. Although now based in France, Pommaret remains enraptured by Bhutan and frequently returns to the country for work and pleasure.

C O N T E N T S

*Pages 2/3:
Tashichho Dzong,
the Fortress of
Auspicious Religion*

Pages 8/9:
a masked dancer at
festival time

HISTORY & CULTURE

Geographical Outline

Bhutan, approximately the size of Switzerland, covers an area of 47,000 sq km (18,147 sq miles), and has a population of less than 700,000. These figures, however, do not reflect the incredible geographical and ecological diversity of the country, nor its natural wealth. Rising from 300m (1,000ft) on the Indian frontier to 7,300m (14,000ft) on the Tibetan (Chinese) border, and in less than 150km (90 miles) as the crow flies, the land is reminiscent of a gigantic staircase.

There are two ways to describe the geography of Bhutan – vertically and horizontally. Vertically, the rivers flow north to south, forging deep valleys through the Himalayan range. Each is separated from the next by lofty ridges, the highest being the Black Mountains, which effectively divide Bhutan into the western, central and eastern regions. Horizontally, the country is divided into four zones. The southern region, rising from 300m to 1,000m (1,000ft to 3,300ft), is tropical in climate and vegetation, and abounds with orange, banana and cardamom plantations. Thick jungles with occasional forest clearings separate the southern belt from the central valleys. These constitute the sub-tropical zone

Laya Lingshi

from 1,200m to 1,600m (4,000ft to 5,250ft), populated in the east and the centre by people who live on forest products and crops of rice, millet and maize. The central valleys are dedicated to agriculture and range from 1,300m to 2,700m (4,300ft to 9,000ft). Depending on the elevation, farmers grow maize, rice, barley, wheat or buckwheat. Apples and potatoes are important cash crops in this area.

These valleys are the core of Bhutanese culture. Dominated by impressive fortresses known as dzongs, Bhutanese houses with their typical trefoil-shape windows and pitched roofs stand among the cultivated fields. Forests of oak, conifer and rhododendron cloak the higher slopes. Small urban centres which cater to a largely agrarian population dot the landscape. A winding, spectacular central road links the different valleys, from Ha in the west to Tashigang in the east, crossing mountain ranges over passes as high as 4,000m (13,000ft). The central valleys are the land of beautiful monasteries and breathtaking temples, of fluttering prayer flags and of exciting contests of archery, the national sport of Bhutan.

Above 3,000m (10,000ft) is the highest ecological zone, dominated by bamboo and coniferous forests, with fir, larch, cypress and pine. This is the domain of yaks, tended by stalwart semi-nomads who during the summer

Archery, the national sport

months graze their charges in upland pastures of 5,000m (16,500ft) and above, living in windswept black tents. Towering over the valleys, clear lakes and meadows of alpine flowers and rare medicinal herbs, the summits of the Himalayan chain form a formidable natural boundary with the Tibetan region of China to the north.

Gigantic spurs radiating southward from this great Himalayan backbone make up the Inner Himalayan Ranges, the mountains and ridges of which form watersheds between the four main river systems of Bhutan: Amochhu (or Torsa), Wang Chu, Puna Tsang Chu, and Manas.

Relatively heavy rains during summer bring precipitation down onto the steep narrow valleys, making it possible to develop small, medium and large hydro-electric projects which produce power for domestic consumption as well as for export to India. In 1996, hydro-electric exports amounted to one-third of Bhutan's total foreign earnings even though less than two percent of its estimated 20,000 megawatt potential had been tapped. The Bhutanese government sees hydro-electric power as a sustainable and environmentally clean source of revenue for its important development and conservation projects.

Monks at Tashichho Dzong

Druk Yul, Bhutan's official name in the Dzongkha language, is usually translated as the Land of the Dragon and is always explained by a traditional story. When the saint Tsangpa Gyare

Yeshe Dorje was consecrating a new monastery in Tibet at the end of the 12th century, he heard thunder, commonly believed to be the voice of the dragon, *druk*. Tsangpa decided to name his monastery Druk, and the religious school which he founded as Drukpa. When the Drukpas unified the country in the 17th century, they decided to name it after themselves.

The origin of the name Bhutan is unclear, but the most logical guess is that it comes from the Indian term Bhotanta, which refers to regions bordering Tibet.

Origins of the People

Festival gathering

About 70 percent of the country is inhabited by the Drukpas, people of Mongoloid descent who migrated from Tibet. Although the difficulties of terrain favoured the development of distinct local characteristics and languages in the past, the social development of Bhutan today is geared towards the creation of 'One Nation, One People'. Dzongkha, the national language, is related to the Tibetan language and is a compulsory subject at school, although English is the medium of instruction.

The southern lowlands are mostly inhabited by people of Nepali origins and account for about 30 percent of the population. These people have been migrating to Bhutan since the end of the 19th century and all those settled prior to 1958 have Bhutanese citizenship. Because of differences in language and religion, they have not assimilated well with the Drukpas.

Since 1959, immigration from Nepal has been banned. The 1988

A mural of the saint, Guru Rinpoche

census led to the eviction of a number of 'illegal immigrants', although many Nepalese had been living in Bhutan for decades. Combined with the 'One Country, One People' policy intended to strengthen national unity, the eviction has created resentment in the south and led to the departure of thousands of ethnic Nepalese from Bhutan, some of whom have set up pro-democracy movements in Kathmandu. The Drukpa population remains committed to the king and his policy as being essential to the survival of Bhutan.

History of the Southern Valleys

Although its history can be traced to ancient times, Bhutan's unification dates only from the middle of the 17th century. Known since the 7th century in Tibetan texts as the Southern Valleys, Bhutan was for centuries a series of independent valleys ruled by rival chieftains.

Bhutan was converted to Buddhism in the 8th century by the great saint Padmasambhava, also known as Guru Rinpoche, which means Precious Master. From the 11th century onwards, religious preachers came from Tibet and settled in Bhutan. They propagated their own religious schools and became, through alliances and marriages, a ruling elite with spiritual and secular powers. This emergent religious nobility controlled west Bhutan. In the central and eastern parts of the country, however, they shared power with the old aristocracy.

The giant thangka at Paro Tsechu

The most important of the new denominations was the Drukpa Kagyudpa school, whose teachings were propagated in west Bhutan as early as the 13th century by Phajo Drugom Shigpo (1184–1251), and the Nyingmapa sect, which had great influence in central and east Bhutan, especially through the saint Pemalingpa (1450–1521) and his descendants.

In 1616, a great religious leader of the Drukpa Kagyudpa school in Tibet, the Shabdrung Ngawang Namgyel (1594–1651), took refuge in Bhutan. With his religious power and strong sense of politics, Namgyel transformed the Southern Valleys into a unified country called Druk Yul. He set up a central administration, established a legal system, built many dzongs and strengthened the Drukpa clergy. Namgyel left such a strong imprint on Bhutanese history that the political system he created lasted until 1907 when Ugyen Wangchuck, the first king of Bhutan, was crowned and the Wangchuck dynasty founded.

Under the Wangchucks, Bhutan entered the 20th century whilst retaining its independence. The third king, Jigme Dorje Wangchuck (1952–1972) is known as the Father of Modern Bhutan because of development plans he initiated, including Bhutan's admittance to the United Nations in 1971. The present monarch, His Majesty King Jigme Singye Wangchuck, carries on the improvements of his father, with added concern for the environment and the preservation of Bhutanese culture.

Until the 1970s, Bhutan had very limited contact with the West, its geography greatly contributing to its isolation. The Bhutanese fought the Duar War against the British over the southern belt in 1865. The years to follow saw a remarkable warming of Anglo-Bhutanese relations, and this friendly association continued with India after its independence. Indian assistance proved crucial in the early stages of the modernisation of the country, and the establishment of links with many

Mask dance

Etiquette

Bhutanese etiquette is so complex a tradition that it can fill volumes. Remember that a large part of discovering new cultures is appreciating different customs, even if sitting cross-legged on the floor for hours is not your idea of fun. The following is a short survival kit.

The Bhutanese are an easy-going, polite and smiling people but these gentle qualities should not mislead the visitor into behaving carelessly or indiscreetly. Although generally amiable, they are an intensely proud people and have fiercely defended their independence, culture and traditions over the years. The highest compliment you can pay the Bhutanese is to respect their culture and try to understand their sensibilities.

When you visit temples, dzongs and monasteries, do not speak too loudly as it violates the sanctity of the site. A small donation of a few Ngultrums should be left on the altar. Always pass a *chorten* (stupa) on your right and go clockwise around all religious monuments.

Religious people, elders and officials are treated with honour. Pay them deference by letting them speak first and stand up when they enter a room.

Take off your shoes when you enter a temple, and also in private houses, if you observe the Bhutanese doing so. Hats and scarfs should be taken off in dzongs (fortresses) and monasteries, and smoking is never allowed.

If you have no spiritual convictions, keep your opinions to yourself. The Bhutanese are a devout and religious people and there is no need to shock them by expressing views that they will not comprehend.

The thumbs-up sign or pointing with a finger is considered very impolite in Asia. Beckon with all your fingers together, palm downwards. Likewise, use only your right hand to give or accept any object, especially food. The left hand is considered polluted in Asia.

Touching others, and especially someone of the opposite sex, is not courteous. If you sit on the floor, sit cross-legged or with your legs folded on one side. Never point your feet at another person.

Avoid getting angry in any situation. Try to keep cool and tackle problems in a courteous manner which will benefit both parties.

It is customary to leave your host's house as soon as the meal or refreshment is finished. Do not linger on. If you visit remote villages, carry your own drinking cup. Hospitality demands that you be served drinks thrice. Just take a small sip each time and your cup will be replenished.

You are expected to refuse your host at least once when you are offered food or drink. After the first formal resistance, you may then accept. Likewise, you must respond by insisting if you are serving a guest.

Gifts are a much more an integral part of Bhutanese life than in Western society. Presents are always given wrapped and should never be opened on the spot or in front of the giver.

Bring with you a selection of presents in case you have to reciprocate; perfume, make-up and pantyhose for ladies, ball-pens for kids and knee-length argyle stockings and knives for the men.

To avoid making unnecessary blunders, it's safer to watch others and follow what they do. When you realise that you have done something wrong, do not hesitate to apologise.

countries and the United Nations has given Bhutan the opportunity to be better known in the international arena. The open policy has also helped the country receive assistance in numerous progressive fields at home.

The Monarchy

Bhutan is ruled by a monarchy. His Majesty King Jigme Singye Wangchuck is the Head of State. The king is assisted by a cabinet, comprising his ministers and some high officials, the chairman of which is the Head of Government. The cabinet is the main executive body of the government.

The National Assembly was created in 1953 and has 150 members, with meetings twice a year in Thimphu. The Royal Advisory Council, set up in 1965, is a counselling body to the king. The council is always in session and has nine members, approved by the National Assembly. The judicial system is headed by the king, to whom any Bhutanese can appeal. District courts are presided by a High Court in Thimphu and litigants plead their own case, or seek representation by *Jabmi*, traditionally a community elder. The country is divided into 20 districts, each headed by a *Dzongdag*, appointed by the king and responsible to the Home Ministry. At the village level is the headman, the *Gup*, who is selected by the villagers and acts as a middleman between them and the government.

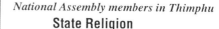

State Religion

The Drukpa Kagyudpa religious school of Buddhism is the state religion of Bhutan. It is a branch of the Tantric Buddhism of Tibet which itself sprouted from Mahayana Buddhism or the Great Vehicle. The word 'Tantrism' comes from Tantra, a corpus of esoteric texts which appeared between the 3rd and 10th centuries. Adherents aim to attain enlightenment, which is the release from the endless cycle of incarnations into the state of *nirvana*, thus annihilating the state of suffering which accompanies all existence.

To understand the complex theological texts, the student of Buddhism needs a *guru*, or teacher. A *lama* is a religious master who leads his disciple through a series of initiations and practices to a higher level of understanding. To reach the highest levels of learning takes many years of study and much discipline. There are presently about 3,500 ordained monks, or *gelong*, in Bhutan who are supported by the state. They fall under the authority of the Je Khenpo, the head of all religious affairs, who presides over the monastic organisation, the Dratshang Lhentshog. In addition, there are another 3,000 monks who are not supported by the state but live under private patronage. There are a further 15,000 lay priests, called *gomchen*, who mostly follow the Nyingmapa sect and do not belong to the main body of monks. The Nyingmapa sect of Buddhism is especially strong in central and eastern Bhutan.

The Bhutanese are very pious and the religion practised at the people's level consists of worshipping the Buddha, Guru Rinpoche and the deities of the Tantric pantheon, as well as numerous indigenous gods. In formal worship, an image of the Buddha symbolises his body, a stupa his speech, and a scripture-book his enlightened mind. Rituals are performed at all significant occasions. Daily prayers are said in front of the family altar, holy *mantras* (chants) are recited with rosaries, butter lamps are offered in the temples, prayer flags are erected, and nobody would miss the opportunity of a blessing from a high lama. Undertaking pilgrimages, sponsoring collective blessings, and the construction or restoration of temples are activities which are regarded as being meritorious.

Prayer wheels

The Economy

Nearly half of the Gross National Product (GNP) of Bhutan is based on agriculture, forestry and livestock, with 90 percent of the population dependent on these sectors for their livelihood. Some 95 percent of the Bhutanese own land; maize is the most important crop, with rice a close second. The fastest growing sectors are light industries, trade, electricity production and mining (dolomite, limestone, gypsum, coal and slate). Bhutan's imports are mostly foodstuff, machinery and oil products, with India as its principal trading partner. The country's exports comprise timber, minerals, cement, agricultural products, canned fruit juice and jam, alcoholic beverages and hydro-electricity.

The national airline, Druk Air, tourism and the sale of novelty stamps made of silk or metal are important sources of foreign exchange but constitute only a small part of the GNP. Tourism is controlled and only a small number of tourists are allowed into the country each year.

The approach to modernisation is cautious, with environmental concerns carefully integrated into development plans. Over 60 percent of the country is legislated to remain under permanent forest cover, and parks and reserves comprise over 22 percent of the land area. Conservation of natural resources is given priority over their commercial exploitation.

Monk at prayer

Historical Highlights

7th century Bhutan is first mentioned in Tibetan texts as the Southern Valleys. Two Buddhist temples, Kyichu in the Paro valley and Jampey in Bumthang, are built by Tibetan King Songtsengampo.

8th century Guru Rinpoche, founder of the Nyingmapa sect, visits Bhutan and Buddhism spreads.

9th–10th century Unknown period in Bhutan following the assassination of the anti-Buddhist Tibetan King Langdarma in 842 and the collapse of the monarchy in Tibet. Important population immigration probably takes place at this time.

11th century Revival of Buddhism and religious activities.

12th century The Lhapa Kagyudpa sect is founded in west Bhutan.

13th century Phajo Drugom Shigpo establishes the Drukpa Kagyudpa school in west Bhutan and clashes with the Lhapa Kagyudpas for power.

14th–16th century Period of intense religious activity. Many sects settle in west Bhutan but the Drukpa Kagyudpa emerge as spiritually and politically pre-eminent. Power remains in the hands of local nobility in central and east Bhutan, where Nyingmapa is the most important religious school.

17th century The Drukpa Kagyudpa heirarch, the Shabdrung Ngawang Namgyel, flees Tibet in 1616 and unifies Bhutan. He defeats religious opponents, repels Tibetan invasions, builds fortresses throughout the country and institutes a legal system based on Buddhist precepts. A dual system of government under Drukpa Kagyudpa hegemony is established.

18th century Internal problems lead to civil strife. Two British missions enter Bhutan to find out more about their isolated northern neighbour and establish trade routes.

19th century Internal dissension continues until the middle of the century when the Tongsa Penlog (governor) Jigme Namgyel comes to power.

1864–1865 Duar War with the British. Bhutan exchanges a fertile southern strip of land for monetary compensation. The Treaty of Sinchula marks the beginning of good relations with the British.

1881 Ugyen Wangchuck succeeds his father as Tongsa Penlop and carries on his work.

1885 Resistance from the Thimphu and Punakha fortresses is crushed at the Battle of Changlimithang.

1907 Tongsa Penlop Ugyen Wangchuck is crowned first king of Bhutan on 17th December 1907. Bhutanese are sent to Western-run schools in Darjeeling and Kalimpong.

1949 Treaty of Friendship and Assistance with India.

1952 Third King Jigme Dorje Wangchuck ascends the throne. Establishes the National Assembly, the High Court in 1968 and Bhutan joins the United Nations in 1971.

1972 Fourth King Jigme Singye Wangchuck ascends the throne at age 17. He continues progressive work whilst trying to encourage the traditional culture. He also initiates diplomatic links beyond India.

1974 Bhutan opens its doors to tourists. The first 287 visitors arrive.

1983 Druk-Air, Bhutan's national airline, is inaugurated.

1985 Bhutan joins the South Asian Association for Regional Cooperation.

1989 Bhutan begins its 'One Nation, One People' policy in an attempt to strengthen and preserve the country's cultural heritage.

1990 Political tension between the southern Bhutanese of Nepali origin and the Drukpa mounts, resulting in demonstrations and the departure of thousands of Nepalese.

1998 To democratise government, King Jigme Singye Wangchuck reconstitutes the cabinet, relinquishing some of his own power and appointing the chairman of the cabinet as Head of Government. The king remains as Head of State.

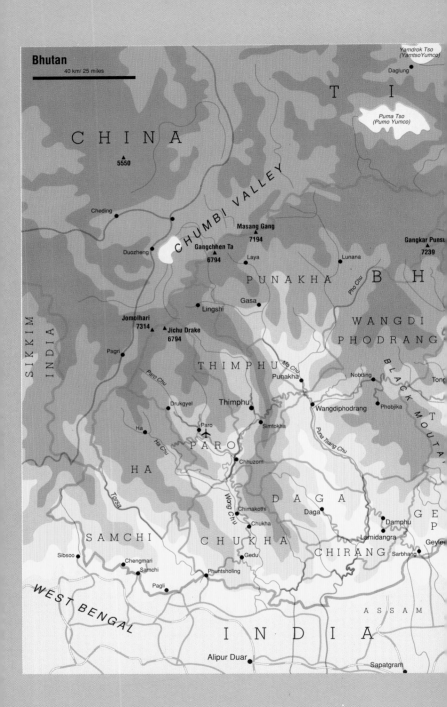

Paro & Thimphu

Paro, at 2,250m (7,382ft), is where you fly into. It offers the calm of the countryside, beautiful landscapes, scenic villages and historic buildings. The valley is large and places of interest are scattered several kilometres apart so count two full days for your visit. There are now several excellent hotels in Paro, including the traditional-style Olathang, hidden among pine trees; the palatial Druk Hotel, built in the dzong (fortress) style and overlooking the valley; and the Japanese-inspired Kyichu Resort, located on the way to Drukgyel Dzong. Paro offers a limited choice of restaurants and evening entertainment, but then, nobody comes to Bhutan for the nightlife.

Thimphu, at 2,350m (7,710ft), is the capital of the country, a 1½- hour drive from Paro, and a widespread township. It boasts a number of magnificent monuments and is the single most rewarding place to spend time in Bhutan. In Thimphu you will find the best selection of handicrafts and quality fabrics because this is the main market for both the Bhutanese and the tourist.

Plan to devote three days to Thimphu. If you are not in the hands of Bhutan Tourism Corporation or if you are going trekking, add an extra day for errands and preparation. It is best to have at least one weekend in Thimphu because of the attraction of the market. Keep in mind that all shops and a few restaurants now close on Tuesday, although government offices remain open.

Paro Valley Itineraries

4 km / 2.5 miles

Drukgyel Dzong (Ruin)
PARO VALLEY
Bumdra
Chumophug
Taktsang Monastery
3217
Do Chhu
DOLPO VALLEY
Satsam Chorten
Kungachoeling
Kyichu Resort
Sangnag Coekhor
Kyichu Lhakhang
Paro Chhu
Dungtse Lhakhang
2819
Drangyekha
Choeding
Druk
Paro Town
National Museum
Olathang Hotel
Ugyen Pelri Palace
Paro Dzong (Rinpung Dzong)
Zuri Dzong
Gorina
Gantey
Druk Hotel
3375
Internat. Airport
Woochu
Bondey
4118
Thimphu
Dzong Krakha
Cheli La
Ha

····· Itinerary 1
····· Itinerary 2

A rented car is the most convenient way to explore Bhutan and these itineraries – starting from Paro in the west and ending at Tashigang in the east, assume you have arranged one (see *Practical Information*, pg 83). Taxis are few, unreliable and relatively expensive, and the public transport system virtually non-existent. If you are not with a tour group,

Paro valley

you will need to apply for a permit for travel outside Paro and Thimphu, and a second permit to enter restricted dzongs and monasteries of Bhutan. See *Practical Information* pg. 81 for more details. Generally, dzongs and monasteries are open from 8am to dusk; where special conditions and hours apply, this is indicated in the text. Always have with you a warm sweater and a flashlight when going inside as they can be cold and dark.

1. Paro Valley

An introduction to Paro valley. Views of Jomolhari mountain and visits to Drukgyel Dzong, Dungtse Lhakhang, the National Museum, Paro Dzong, Ugyen Pelri Palace and Paro village.

If the weather is fine, leave as early as possible in the morning and drive for about 20 minutes to the end of the valley to Drukgyel Dzong. There are good views of the towering **Jomolhari** (7,314m/23,996ft) from here. This mountain, also revered as a powerful goddess, forms the border with Tibet and provides a magnificent background to the ruined Drukgyel Dzong and its village. If you cannot see Jomolhari, return another morning when the weather improves. It is a sight not to be missed, although likely to be obscured by monsoon clouds from May to October. Just before Drukgyel Dzong, on the left side of the valley, you will see the new **Drukgyel High School**, built with British assistance.

Drukgyel Dzong, the Dzong of the Victorious Drukpas, was built in the 1650s to commemorate victory over the Tibetan armies and to guard Paro valley against further aggressions. In 1951, the dzong caught fire and was never repaired except for the shingled roof erected in 1985. The dzong is now an empty shell, a place to meditate on the past.

The tarred road ends here and continues as a small path to the northern border area of Lingshi, home of yak herders. Spend about an hour walking a little way along this trail. The countryside is beautiful and you will meet horsemen coming to trade in Paro. The view of the ruins is more evocative than from the Paro side and you will understand better the defensive purpose of Drukgyel Dzong.

On the way back to Paro village, about 6km (4 miles) from

The ruins of Drukgyel Dzong

Drukgyel Dzong, is a mansion on the right. This is the **Ugyen Wangchuck Academy,** where the present king went to school. On the left across the river is the holy monastery of Taktsang (see *Itinerary 2*), nestling in its eyrie on the large black cliff face. A few kilometres on the right, a cluster of prayer flags signals the temple of **Kyichu Lhakhang** (closed to visitors). The temple dates back to the 7th century when, according to Bhutanese legend, Songtsengampo, the first Buddhist king of Tibet, established a temple here on the left knee of an ogress in order to subdue her. The temple was restored in the 19th century and a second temple, in the same style, was added in 1968 by Ashi Kesang, the Queen Mother of Bhutan.

If feeling the effects of altitude and jet lag, go back to your hotel for a quiet lunch. For simple fare in Paro town, try the Chinese food at **Sonam Trophel**, which caters to Western tastes. The **Rinpung** and **Highland** restaurants are other possibilities for the more adventurous. Take it easy and drink as much liquid as you can to help your body acclimatise, and avoid alcohol on your first day.

After lunch, leave around 1.45pm and go to the National Museum. The drive will take 20 minutes because the car has to take a circuitous route through Paro town and across the bridge over the Paro river. After the bridge, note **Dungtse Lhakhang** on the left. This little chorten-shaped temple is said to have been established in 1421 by Thangton Gyelpo, who supposedly built the temple on top of an ogress's head to subdue her. It was restored in 1841 by the 25th Head Abbot of Bhutan, Sherab Gyaltsen, and the names of the Paro donors can be seen on the wooden pillars of the ground floor.

This temple is unique in Bhutan as its paintings show the pro-

The terraced fields of Paro

gressive stages of Tantric Buddhist philosophy as well as the most important deities and figures of the Drukpa Kagyudpa school. Conceived as a *mandala*, a mystical diagram of the path to initiation, the temple has three floors. The ground floor is devoted to historical figures, bodhisattvas and deities of wealth and protection. In the inner sanctum are the five Buddhas of meditation and the different forms of the Goddess of Compassion Chenrezi (Avalokiteshwara). On the first floor are the different forms of Yeshe Gonpo (Mahakala), the great protective deity of Bhutan, as well as scenes from *Bardo*, the intermediary state between life and death. Deities of the highest Tantric teachings and those of the Drukpa Kagyudpa lineage occupy the second and third floors. On the top floor, make sure you see the splendid lacquered wood image of the 12th-century saint and poet Milarepa.

Kyichu Lhakhang

Continue to **Dopchari**, a very fertile part of the Paro valley with many houses scattered through the countryside. After crossing another bridge the road ascends past the **Paro Junior High School** on the right. At last you reach the top of the hill. In spring, you will be greeted by yellow forsythias and a sharp wind.

At the entrance of the **National Museum** (Tuesday to Saturday 9am–4pm, Sunday 11am–4pm; closed on some national holidays) notice the large iron chains which come from bridges built by the famous 15th-century saint known as Thangton Gyelpo, or Chagzampa, the Iron Bridge Builder.

It is cool and dark inside the museum, so don't forget your sweater and a flashlight. Housed in a 17th-century watchtower, the building has a unique character and beautiful panoramic views over Paro valley. Opened in 1968, the museum has a good collection of fine arts, paintings and bronzes. There are also textile, jewellery, and handicraft sections as well as galleries of stuffed animals and butterflies indigenous to Bhutan. The stamp hall is very popular and has exhibits like embossed and 3-dimensional stamps, silk stamps and the famous triangular stamp depicting the yeti. The top floor of the museum is a chapel containing a 'tree' depicting the main figures of the four religious schools of Tibetan Buddhism.

After the museum, unless you are tired or it is raining, take the 10-minute walk to **Paro Dzong** where there are good views over the fortress whose structure and layout you can clearly make out. If you drive down, note the amazing cantilever bridge. Unless you have a special permit, it is not possible to enter Paro Dzong.

Also known as Rinpung Dzong, the Fortress of the Heap of Jewels, Paro Dzong was built in 1645 by the Shabdrung Ngawang Namgyel on the site of a smaller 15th-century fort. It was badly damaged by fire in 1907 and immediately restored by the governor of the time. Paro Dzong, an imposing five-storey tall square fortress, is representative of typical dzong architecture, with a central tower and courtyards housing the administrative quarters and the monastic section. Today, the dzong is the seat of the district administration (*dzongkhag*) and has a community of 200 monks.

Pass the dzong and walk down the slope to the **cantilever bridge**. Don't miss seeing the huge beehives hanging from the roof. The bridge is one of the finest specimens in Bhutan with its shingle roof and two guard-houses at each end. You can also see the royal **Ugyen Pelri Palace**, built around 1930 by the governor, Tshering Penjor and based on the heavenly palace of Guru Rinpoche. If you decide to walk down, meet your car beside the huge white chortens (stupas) which mark the alley leading to the village. Better still, send the car ahead and walk the length of this splendid alley, along the wall of the Ugyen Pelri Palace.

Paro village as it exists today is relatively new, dating back only from the mid-1980s. The houses are new but built in the traditional style and richly decorated. The open spaces, the shops lining the one-street village, the wind and swirling dust, horses loaded with wares and their rough-looking owners swaggering out of little bars, all contribute to the strange feeling that you have just stepped into a Wild West town.

Enjoy the shops for their ambience. Try Druk Handicrafts for souvenirs, but don't expect too much from the other shops. The

The bridge to Paro Dzong

Handmade fabrics for sale at the market

weekly market is worth a visit if you are in Paro on a Sunday morning. In spring and autumn, you may see archery contests which are lively events involving lots of shouting and dancing. However, beware of the arrows; it is 120m (400ft) between the archers and their target and as they alternate ends, you may not realise that you are standing next to a target!

If you have time and energy, request a Bhutanese friend or your guide to arrange a visit to a Bhutanese house. Don't forget to take some biscuits or beer as a gift for your host. Or, if you have the stamina, take a 30-minute walk to the old village of **Drangyekha**, perched on a little hillock above the Olathang Hotel.

Alternatively, if the weather is good or it is springtime, drive to Cheli La at 3,780m (12,400ft), separating Paro from the Ha valley, one of the highest road passes in Bhutan. The road starts from Woochu village near Bondey Farm (see map on pg. 22). The 1-hour drive through oak and pine forest is very pleasant, especially in April and May when the rhododendrons are in bloom. If you're lucky

Black Hat dance

enough to be at the top of the pass in clear weather, there is a fantastic view of Jomolhari mountain and the high Himalaya.

Spend the evening at the hotel, catching up with writing postcards and diaries and sampling more Bhutanese food. The only after-dinner entertainment is a drink at the bar, so you will have ample time to rediscover the joys of going to bed early.

2. Taktsang and on to Thimphu

Excursion to Taktsang, the Tiger's Nest, one of the most sacred places in Bhutan and a pilgrimage that every Bhutanese dreams of accomplishing. After a picnic lunch, freshen up at the hotel before the drive from Paro to Thimphu, your base for the next few days.

The excursion to Taktsang Monastery is one of the highlights of a Bhutan visit, although the 3-hour climb may be strenuous for some. The less agile can make arrangements for a horse at the hotel desk or with the guide; otherwise stop at the café two-thirds of the way up to rest your legs. Leave the hotel around 8.30am and don't forget to bring your sweater, hat, sunscreen, water-bottle and some food for sustenance along the way. A 15-minute drive brings you to the flat area from where you start your hike to **Taktsang Monastery** (see map on pg. 22), perched on the edge of a 800m (2,600ft) cliff high above Paro Valley.

After crossing a bridge, the trail glides gently up through fields and forest. You will pass a Bhutanese open-air bath and a lovely shrine where a prayer wheel revolves with the flow of the stream, the little bell tinkling at every turn. After passing a pasture, the path climbs through a forest of oak, pine and rhododendron. Much puffing and panting later, you will reach a big rock surrounded by dozens of prayer flags. The cafe is only three minutes to the right, a nice log cabin hidden in the forest where you can rest and buy some refreshments. Make sure you order lunch as well so it will be ready on your way back.

The view of Taktsang Monastery is ample reward for the trouble you took walking up. And because Taktsang is a pilgrimage site, the locals believe that suffering on the way helps wash away your sins. Several temples make up Taktsang, the most famous being **Taktsang Pelphug**.

If you possibly can, push on another 30 minutes to a spectacular spot at 3,000m (10,000ft) overlooking Taktsang. The walk up through the forest whose trees are festooned with hanging lichens gives you the eerie feeling of having strayed into a fairy tale. Suddenly, the path levels and you reach a saddle. Just across the abyss is the object of your walk, the Taktsang Monastery. You feel you could almost jump onto the monastery roof. If you have an entry permit, allow an extra two hours to visit the monastery. The last stretch of the path, with a difficult climb along a precipitous cliff, is definitely not recommended for those prone to vertigo.

Taktsang, or the Tiger's Nest, owes its name to the 8th-century saint Padmasambhava, who, according to myth, visited here on a flying tiger. Also known as Guru Rinpoche, he subdued the local deities and converted Paro to Buddhism. Guru Rinpoche is said to have meditated in the cave, now the lower floor of the monastery, and is enshrined in his fierce aspect as Dorje Droloe standing on a tiger.

Before arriving at the steep flight of stairs leading into the monastery, the trail dips and makes a bend where, hidden from above, a waterfall cascades 60m (197ft) to a sacred pool beside the path. The pool is believed to have formed miraculously after Guru Rinpoche's consort, Yeshe Tshogyal, flung her rosary on the spot.

Some 20m (66ft) above you on the left is an old meditation hut that seems organically joined to the sheer rock, and, where, even as you pass beneath, a devout monk or lay person will be in solitary retreat for a minimum period of exactly three years, three months, three weeks and three days.

The winding route to Takstang

The monastery dates from 1692 when it was constructed by the fourth Desi (Temporal Ruler) of Bhutan, Tenzin Rabgye. It was restored in the second half of the 19th century and again in 1983, then partly damaged in a 1998 fire. There are two temples above the holy cave. The middle one has an exquisite painting of Guru Rinpoche, his two consorts and the Eight Manifestations. The main statue also represents him and is said to have spoken whilst being carried enroute to Taktsang. A statue of Guru Rinpoche with his Eight Manifestations is also found in the upper temple. Murals here depict the deities which symbolise the esoteric religious cycles of Gondu and Phurpa, originally taught by Guru Rinpoche.

Above the main building, three small temples nestle against the cliff. One is dedicated to Guru Rinpoche as Dorje Droloe, the second to Tshepamey, the Buddha of Infinite Life, and the final one to Namthoese, the God of Wealth. Before leaving the Taktsang Pelphug, visit the room on the right of the dark entrance staircase. The funeral chorten of Pelkyi Sengye, one of the main disciples of Guru Rinpoche, is enshrined here. Once you've seen enough, either picnic in the forest if you have brought food along, or have your pre-ordered meal at the cafe on the way back.

Arriving at the hotel, take a well-earned rest before the journey to Thimphu, a 1½-hour drive with interesting sites on the way. About 2km (1¼ miles) after crossing the Bondey Bridge past the turning to the airport is the **Dzong Krakha**, high on a cliff to the right. This large 14th-century monastic complex boasts a chorten said to have moved by itself. An interesting festival is held here at

Thimphu in the thick of winter

the same time as the Paro Serda (see *Calendar of Special Events*).

Further down the valley narrows 6km (4 miles) before the confluence, and **Tachogang**, Temple of the Excellent Horse, appears on a small mound overlooking the river. It was built around 1420 by the Iron Bridge Builder, Thangton Gyelpo, who saw a vision of Chenrezi, the Bodhisattva of Compassion, in the form of a horse. He also built the bridge which was carried away by floods in 1969. Tachogang is a private monastery and it's not possible to visit. **Chhuzom** is the confluence of the Pachu River of Paro and the Wangchu River, which passes through Thimphu. It is also a crossroad marked by the bridge completed in 1991. Coming from Paro, turn left at the bridge. The other road on your right goes to Ha, the westernmost valley of Bhutan. After the bridge, the road right goes south to Phuntsholing on the Indo-Bhutanese border. Turn left to Thimphu, some 45 minutes away.

After driving about 40 minutes you change direction and cross a small bridge. Glance backwards to see the splendid **Simtokha Dzong**, built in 1629 and consecrated in 1631 by the Shabdrung Ngawang Namgyel. Thimphu is 6km (4 miles) further.

Complete administrative errands in Thimphu (make sure this is a weekday, but not a Tuesday if you want to shop), buy stamps at the Post Office, see the Memorial Chorten, then lunch at Benez and Jichu Drakey Bakery. In the afternoon, visit the Indigenous Hospital, the Painting School and the National Library, followed by an evening stroll and dinner at the Druk Hotel.

If travelling independently and not in the care of a travel agent, devote most of this first morning to organising your stay in Thimphu. Things take time to arrange in Bhutan and it is easy to spoil your trip with inadequate preparations. Change money if you need to at the bank, then proceed to the Immigration Office at Tashichho Dzong with two passport pictures to apply for a travel permit to visit Punakha, Wangdiphodrang, Tongsa and Bumthang (see *Itineraries 7,9,10* and *11*). It can take up two days to process the permit. Check the duration of your Bhutanese visa. If you wish to stay longer than what was given to you at the airport, go to the Visa Office at the Ministry of Foreign Affairs in the SAARC building and apply for an extension. If planning to visit restricted dzongs and monasteries in Bhutan, head for the Special Commission for Cultural Affairs for yet another permit. Be forewarned that unless you are a Buddhist, this permit is very hard to come by.

Reconfirm your return air ticket at the Druk Air Office. If you plan to visit Tongsa and Bumthang, go to a travel agency to make room reservations at one of the guesthouses and hire a 4-wheel drive vehicle. If you are planning to trek, make all the arrangements with a travel agency before leaving Thimphu. Visit the **Post Office** to buy as many stamps as you think you'll need, to save time later. You should also purchase the beautiful stamps for which Bhutan is famous at the **Philatelic Bureau** inside the Post Office.

Your lunch at the hotel may be already included if you are part of a tour group, but you may prefer to eat in town and pay yourself. Thimphu presents the best choice of dining possiblities in Bhutan, with a number of decent and inexpensive places. Today, head for **Benez**, a tiny joint on Gatoen Lam. The restaurant is very popular with the locals, and fa-

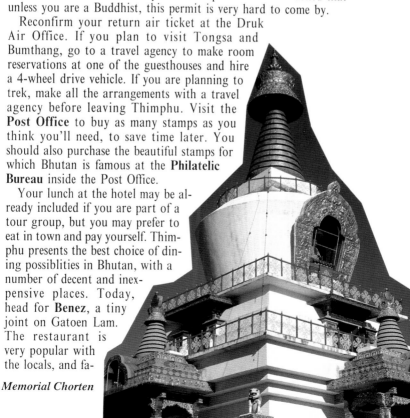

Memorial Chorten

Bookshelves at the National Library

mous for its Tibetan *momos* (meat or cheese dumplings), either fried or steamed. The *thukpa* (noodle soup) and the chow mein are also good. The service is friendly, but don't expect anything fancy.

After lunch, head for the **Jichu Drakey Bakery**, off Chorten Lam, for a good cup of coffee and delicious Viennese-style pastries. The bread and croissants are also excellent. Ugyen, who worked in Austria for five years, is the owner, chief waiter, pastry chef and manager all rolled into one. It is an agreeable place for a break anytime of the day, except between noon and 1.30pm daily when it is closed .

Now work off that lunch by visiting the **Memorial Chorten**, or include it in the morning if time permits. A landmark in Thimphu, the chorten was erected by the Royal Grandmother Ashi Phuntsho Choedron in 1974 in memory of her son the third King Jigme Dorje Wangchuck, who died in 1972. Although his remains are in Kuje Lhakhang in Bumthang, people pay their respects to his photograph mounted on an altar inside the Memorial Chorten. The chorten has great significance in the religious life of the townspeople and symbolises, as do all such monuments, the different levels of the Buddha's mind and teachings. When ritually circumambulated clockwise, one gains merit for the next life and atones for present sins.

The chorten contains three chapels representing the main spiritual themes of the Nyingmapa school, preached by Guru Rinpoche and rediscovered by the great masters, or lamas, Phurpa, Kagye and Lama Gondu. The paintings and sculpture are of excellent quality and reflect the devout faith of the Bhutanese. To gain the most out of your visit, go with a Bhutanese friend or guide who can help interpret the complex esoteric meanings of what you see. If you're lucky, you may see one of the occasional religious ceremonies performed here. The chorten is often filled with worshippers offering fragrant incense, butter for the lamps and white scarfs *(katas)* in order to receive blessings from lamas.

Day Walks in Thimphu

If you are fit and have extra days in Thimphu, there are a number of day walks; Phajoding, Tala, Tashigang Nunnery and Thadra are all recommended. It is always better to go with a Bhutanese guide or friend, however, as the paths are not always obvious and you may encounter wild animals.

If in Thimphu on a weekday, visit the Indigenous Hospital, Painting School and National Library (Monday to Friday 9am–5pm in summer and 9am–4pm in winter: visitors to the hospital are encouraged to make appointnments). Tradi-

A Thimphu grocery shop

tional Bhutanese medicine, a blend of Indian ayurvedic and and Chinese herbal practices, is carried out at the **Indigenous Hospital,** built in 1978. Doctors here test the pulse points and urine of the patients and question them on their way of life and diet. Medicines composed of plants and minerals are prescribed, and sometimes acupuncture or a change of diet. Traditional medicine is actively encouraged by the government and the hospital was developed with aid from an Italian organisation, and, later, the European Union.

Along Chhoephel Lam is the **Painting School**, which is slated for expansion and restoration. Here, children study a course in religious drawing and painting, starting with tiny clouds and finishing, several years later, with exquisite religious paintings called *thangkas.* There are also courses in woodcarving and mask making.

Further along the same road is the **National Library,** established in 1969 and located in a new Bhutanese style building. The museum contains an important collection of foreign books on Bhutan, the Himalaya and Buddhism, and a unique series of Bhutanese and Tibetan books and manuscripts imprinted with woodblocks called xylographs. These traditional Bhutanese prints are done on handmade paper from the pulp of the Daphne shrub. On the upper floor is a collection of the engraved woodblocks. Ask a librarian in the Reading Room to guide your visit.

In the evening, stroll through town and peep into the bay-windows of the shops where you will find typical samples of the town-folk's basic needs: foodstuff, plastic goods and nowadays, video cassettes. One of the most interesting is Shop No 8 on the main street which overflows with Indian and Bhutanese processed foods, vegetables, noodles, flattened maize, rice, eggs, flour and dry cheese. For dinner, go to the poshest restaurant in town at the **Druk Hotel**. The Indian and Continental food here is very good. Have a drink of the local Bhutanese whisky before dinner; either the Special Courier or Royal Supreme Whiskey. Stay away from imported drinks which will fast deplete your pocket.

Engraving a woodblock

Visit the Thimphu Government Handicrafts Emporium and Changangkha Lhakhang before lunch at the Sambara. See the Tashichho Dzong, have tea at the Swiss Bakery and do a little shopping before a Bhutanese dinner at the Hotel Druk Yul.

Leave at about 9am for the **Government Handicrafts Emporium** (summer: daily 9am–6pm; winter: daily 9am–5pm) to get an idea of the range, quality and prices of the handicrafts available. The emporium has a good range of *thangkas*, bamboo crafts, textiles, woodcarving, jewellery, books and pottery. The salespersons are very pleasant and patient. If you cannot decide on anything, wait to see the other shops and come back before 5pm. If planning to shop with credit cards here, note that only American Express cards are accepted.

Drive to **Changangkha Lhakhang**, one of the oldest temples in Thimphu. Changangkha Lhakhang was built in the 15th century by a Bhutanese lama of the Drukpa Kagyudpa school. The temple's silhouette, perched high on a spur, is a landmark of Thimphu. Surprisingly, the first renovations in the temple's long history were only begun in 1993. The repairs, which include the new gold roof, were financed by contributions from the government, business community and other individuals. Although you cannot go inside the temple, sit next to the prayer flag and enjoy the good views over Thimphu valley.

Have lunch today at the trendy (by Bhutanese standards at least!) **Sambara**, a very cosy restaurant on Gatoen Lam. The Chinese food is deliciously spicy.

After lunch, head for **Tashichho Dzong** (summer: Monday to Friday 9am–5pm with a permit; if visiting after 5pm and on weekends, no permit required; winter: open the whole day and no permit required). If you haven't got the requisite permit in summer, save your visit for the weekend as the light is too poor to see the pictures after 5pm. By ancient custom, the State Monastic Community is in residence in Tashichho Dzong during the summer months from April to October. During the winter months from November to March, the monk body migrates to Punakha Dzong (see *Itinerary 7*). When the monks are in residence, no one is allowed to visit these dzongs during daylight hours without special permits.

Before reaching Tashichho Dzong, pass the white structure of the High Court on the left, the golf course and finally some little white cottages which house government offices.

Tashichho Dzong, also known as the Fortress of Auspicious Religion, or Thimphu Dzong, is

Bhutanese crafts

one of the largest in Bhutan, together with Tongsa Dzong (see *Itinerary 9*). Tashichho Dzong was extended in the 1960s to its present form by the third King Jigme Dorje Wangchuck, using traditional techniques and modelled after the original structure. In some places, the dzong's mud walls are 2m (6½ft) thick.

The history of the dzong dates back to 1216 when the first fortress, the Do Ngon Dzong, or the Fort of the Blue Stone, was built by the religious sect of the Lhapa Kagyudpa. Built on a spur above the present Tashichho Dzong, it had a defensive purpose. In 1641, the Shabdrung Ngawang Namgyel took it over, enlarged it and renamed it Tashichho Dzong. The fortress was burnt down in 1772 and was rebuilt where it stands today.

The dzong's imposing size is matched only by the beauty of its decoration. The first courtyard that you enter contains **government ministries**, and the second belongs to the **State Monastic Commu-**

Tashichho Dzong

nity. Between the two courtyards stands the **central tower** and the **Lhakhang Sarpa**, built in 1907. The animals and dwarfs decorating this temple are noteworthy. A building on the north side of the dzong houses the monks' **Assembly Hall** and on the first floor, the former **National Assembly Hall**. Try not to miss this as it is decorated with exquisite paintings on the life of Buddha.

Your visit will take about an hour. When you're done, return to town to shop at private handicraft shops like Ethometho, Tshering Drolkar, Choeki Handicrafts, Druk-Trin Rural Handicrafts and the ICDP Showroom (see the *Shopping* chapter) or go back to the Government Handicrafts Emporium which you visited this morning.

You now deserve a break and a cup of tea at the acclaimed **Swiss Bakery** where the French baguette is excellent. For dinner head to **Hotel Druk Yul** for Bhutanese food or their delicious Tibetan soups combining meat, mushrooms and rice noodles.

5. Thimphu Market and the Countryside

Ensure this is a weekend. Spend the morning shopping at the Thimphu market and watching archery at the Changlimithang Stadium. Lunch at Plum's Cafe, or the 89 Restaurant, then hire a car for the drive through the countryside to Taba and Dechenchoeling. In April/May, continue to Begana to see the rhododendrons in bloom. Dinner at the Jomolhari Hotel Restaurant.

The **Thimphu weekend market** is a must for the visitor. Saturday morning is more interesting for local colour as more people come from the outlying villages. On Sunday, not only are there markedly fewer people, most of the produce would have been sold out. Besides exotic fruit and unknown vegetables, you will find goods that the Bhutanese use in their homes – all manner of baskets, yak hair ropes and blankets, bamboo boxes, wonderful textiles, round white cakes of yeast, minerals for dying cloth, tea in the shape of bricks or cones for salt butter tea, Szechuan pepper, juniper and incense to burn, religious musical instruments, prayer books and images of important lamas. Prices are more or less fixed and you cannot bargain. In August and September, you may be tempted to buy chantarelle mushrooms for as little as US$1.50 per kilo. And the piles of orchids for sale are not to be placed in a vase, but eaten in curry as a great delicacy of Bhutanese cuisine. The meat market is not very salubrious but in November you can see huge chunks of yak meat for sale.

If you happen to be visiting in spring or autumn, watch the **archery competition** from the newly constructed stadium at the south end of Changlimithang. One of the most frustratingly difficult events to photograph, the sight of the archers is extremely impressive for visitors. You can only marvel at the accurate eyesight and deft agility of the Bhutanese men who stand next to the target and avoid, at what seems the very last moment, arrows from over 120m (400ft) away.

Have lunch at **Plum's Cafe**, a bright little place overlooking the

Bamboo baskets at the weekend market

main traffic roundabout on Norzim Lam. Try the excellent Chinese or Thai curries, or the western-style fast food, but save room for their excellent apple pie. If you prefer spaghetti Bolognese or good french fries, go instead to the **89 Restaurant** on Chorten Lam.

This afternoon, explore the countryside around Thimphu by car. First, drive to the **Drubthob Gompa**, a small red monastery with a splendid view just above Tashichho Dzong. Have a look at the red temple built in the early 1980s and at the small attached nunnery.

Take the road north towards Taba and Dechenchoeling. Turn down towards the river, cross the bridge, and turn left. The huge, ornate building just below the road was specially built for a South Asian Association for Regional Cooperation (SAARC) conference, and now houses government offices and the National Assembly Hall, where the 150 Assembly members meet annually to discuss new laws and policy matters with the king and ministers.

The road above the Indian Embassy and paddy fields winds through the forest before reaching the village of **Taba** where Bhutan's **Forestry Institute** has its headquarters. Once a remote rural Bhutanese village, Taba has witnessed a construction boom in recent years and has be-

Lush Dechenchoeling valley

come a much sought-after suburb of Thimphu by the well-to-do.

After Taba, you soon reach **Dechenchoeling**. From the road, you can catch a glimpse of the **Dechenchoeling Royal Palace**, a beautiful mansion set in a heavenly garden. After the bridge and the guard house, turn right to the compound of **Pangri Zampa**. Both these religious buildings were built in the 16th century and became the first residence of the Shabdrung Ngawang Namgyel when he arrived in Thimphu in 1616. The buildings are not open to the public, but the small meadow, huge cypresses, long prayer wall and cascading river give the place an almost magical charm. If you have an hour left and it is April or May, continue north until **Begana** where there is a hydro-electricity project. When in full bloom, the rhododendrons in the forest around Begana are really gorgeous.

On the way back to Thimphu, instead of turning right across the bridge near the Tashichho Dzong, continue along the left bank of the river. From the road is a fine panorama of the town. Return by the Lungtenzampa bridge and the Bhutanese style petrol pump.

Have dinner at the smart **Jomolhari Hotel Restaurant**, where the service can be slow but the Indian food and the sizzlers are very good. Or, enjoy the plush atmosphere of the **Blue Poppy**, next to Swiss Bakery, where you can have red rice and *churu-gondo*, eggs served over edible algae from Bhutan's fast running streams.

Punakha Vallere Wangdiphodrang

The semi-tropical Punakha and Wangdi-phodrang are situated north of one another in the same river valley two hours drive 65km (40 miles) east of Thimphu. Both places enjoy a warm climate and exceptional rice harvests. In former times, Thimphu residents used to migrate to the milder climes of Punakha or Wangdiphodrang in winter, a practice the monastic community still continues today. Many civil servants from Thimphu for instance visit their village at Punakha or Wangdiphodrang during weekends. In turn, valley farmers bring in their chillies, oranges and betel leaves to Thimphu's weekly market. Many people own houses and land in each valley. Improved communications and the completion of the road have further fostered this close relationship.

If visiting Punakha and Wangdiphodrang from May to October, wear long-sleeved shirts and trousers to protect against mosquitoes, leeches and sandflies. Carry insect repellent and antihistamine ointment to prevent bites from turning septic.

6. Simtokha Dzong and on to Mendegang

Visit Simtokha Dzong before climbing Dochu La pass for mountain vistas. Descend to the Punakha/Wangdiphodrang valley and spend the night at Mendegang.

Book your room at the **Dechen Cottages** in Mendegang before leaving Thimphu as there are only four cottages. Although relatively expensive, do not miss the opportunity to have a stone bath in this Bhutanese-style cottage.

Details from a monastery wall

Simtokha Dzong

The alternatives are **Gantey Thanka**, **Kyichu Resort**, and **Dragon's Nest** in Wangdiphodrang, or, **Zangtho Pelri Hotel** in Punakha.

Leave Thimphu on the Wangdiphodrang road from where there is a good view of **Simtokha Dzong**, worth a visit if you have the permit. Built in 1629 by the Shabdrung Ngawang Namgyel, Simtokha was the first dzong he built after arriving in Bhutan. The dzong is built on a strategic position on a hill commanding the crossroads of the Paro, Thimphu and Punakha roads. Inside, behind the prayer wheels that encircle the central tower, is an unusual collection of engraved slates depicting deities and other religious figures. The main temple contains the largest 17th-century statues in Bhutan. The images represent Sakyamuni, the Historical Buddha with his two main disciples and eight *bodhisattvas*. The small chapel on the left is dedicated to Chenrezi, the Bodhisattva of Compassion, and has exquisite paintings of Drukpa Kagyudpa lamas. The dzong is a living monastery where monks reside, study and pray. Nearby is a secular school for the study of the Dzongkha language.

The road climbs steeply for 45 minutes to the **Dochu La pass** at 3,116m (10,023ft) through oak, pine and rhododendron forests. Stop at **Hongtso** to show your travel permit. Dochu La is marked with a large square chorten and a wind-blown cluster of prayer flags. In winter or exceptionally clear weather, the view is stunning. To get here as early as possible you might consider saving Simtokha Dzong for your return journey.

From left to right is the **Masang Gang** (7,194m/13,602ft) above the Laya region, followed by the **Tsendagang** (6,994m/22,946ft), the **Terigang** (7,094m/23,274ft), the **Jejegangphugang** (7,194m/23,602ft), the **Kangphugang** (7,170m/23,524ft), the **Zongaphugang** (7,060m/23,163ft) and finally **Gangkar Punsum** (7,239m/23,750ft), the highest peak in Bhutan.

From Dochu La, the road descends through different vegetation to the Punakha/Wangdiphodrang valley at 1,300m (4,300ft). The magnolia and rhododendron forest is an unforgettable sight from mid-March to end April. The trees become more tropical towards the village of **Thinleygang**. Several kilometres on, you arrive at **Mendegang**; on the right is a board announcing **Dechen Cottages**.

Visit the old capital of Punakha, taking in its dzong and the Machan Lhakhang. Onward to windswept Wangdiphodrang.

Leave Mendegang about 8.30am with a picnic lunch. Notice the distinctive round shape of the chir pine trees on the one-hour drive to Punakha. It is difficult to believe that this sleepy village was the old capital, but the historical importance of the Punakha Dzong is what counted in ancient Bhutan. As villages were never built around fortresses back then, Punakha village only dates from the 1980s when the **High School** was first established.

The riverside Punakha Dzong

From a spot just below the school gate, there is a good view of **Punakha Dzong** (open in summer; permit required in winter) at 1,350m (4,430ft) looking like a huge ship at the confluence of two rivers, the Mochu and the Phochu.

Built in 1637 by the Shabdrung Ngawang Namgyel, the site however is much older; the 1328 temple of saint Ngagi Rinchen can still be seen opposite the main dzong, called the **Dzongchung** or Little Dzong. In 1994, a glacial lake outburst in Lunana caused a flash flood to sweep down the Phochu. Although the eastern wall of the Dzongchung was torn away, the sacred statue of Buddha just inside the wall was miraculously untouched.

Punakha Dzong was restored twice in the 17th century. It was damaged six times by fire, once by floods and once by earthquake. Bhutan's first king, Ugyen Wangchuck, was crowned here. The dzong is the winter residence of the Central Monastic Community and the administrative headquarters of the Punakha district.

Festival at Wangdiphodrang

Monks' courtyard at Punakha

Opposite the entrance gate, note the legal code inscribed on slates by an edict of the Shabdrung Ngawang Namgyel. The chorten in the first courtyard was built in 1981. The dzong contains a total of 21 temples, all of which are closed to visitors. The most important, the **Machan Lhakhang**, enshrines the mummified body of the Shabdrung Ngawang Namgyel who died while in retreat here in 1651. The monks' **Assembly Hall** is in the last courtyard. The great Punakha Serda festival takes place every year at the end of winter (see *Calendar of Special Events*).

Take the road north of the dzong up the beautiful Mochu valley with its sandy riverbank and old farmhouses set in terraced fields. There are many nice places to stop and have your picnic.

Half an hour from Punakha is Wangdiphodrang, known colloquially as Wangdi. Cross the bridge that was originally built in 1685 and look out for the scenic village of **Rinchengang**, huddling on a vertical hillside and famous for its stone masons. Buffeted by afternoon winds, Wangdi is an important stop on the road east, but food and accommodation are very basic. The impressive **Wangdiphodrang Dzong** houses the provincial monastic community and can only be seen with a special permit. It was built in 1638 by the Shabdrung Ngawang Namgyel and enlarged in 1683 by the fourth Temporal Ruler of Bhutan, Tenzin Rabgye. The silver shingled roof, narrow courtyards and tranquil ambience give it a very special feeling. After Wangdiphodrang either return to Mendegang, drive back two hours to Thimphu or push on east another four hours to Tongsa.

8. Phobjika Valley

Visit spectacular Phobjika valley, home of the Gantey Gompa, and the rare black-necked crane from November to April.

This itinerary is only recommended from October to May because the road to Phobjika valley is usually blocked by landslides during the summer monsoon months. Don't forget your down jacket as you'll need it.

Leave Wangdiphodrang about 7am with a packed lunch and hit the road for Tongsa. After 2½ hours on this spectacular route, you reach Phobjika at 3,000m (10,000ft) in the **Black Mountains**, the highest of Bhutan's north-south ridges. The unmarked turning right off the Tongsa road towards Phobjika is 7km (4½ miles) after the nondescript village of Nobding, 40km (25 miles) from Wangdi. The only landmark is a large farmhouse with a flat field

Gantey Gompa

in front of it just before the junction. The road ascends for about 10km (6 miles) through a rhododendron forest grazed in winter and early spring by herds of yaks. After going past a mountain pass, the contrast of the open, marshland **Phobjika valley** is striking.

Gantey Gompa, the main attraction of Phobika valley, is built on a small knoll. This Nyingmapa monastery looks like a dzong and was founded in the late 16th century by Pema Trinley, the grandson of Pemalingpa, the great Bhutanese saint of Bumthang. At the end of the 17th century it was enlarged to its present dimensions by the second incarnation, the Abbot Tenzin Legpey Dondrup. Today, headed by the 9th reincarnation, Gantey Gompa is no longer private property and permission is needed to visit. Known for its lovely paintings and statues, Gantey Gompa is ringed with family houses of the *gomchen*, the religious laymen who worship and work at the monastery.

After your picnic lunch (find a sheltered place away from the icy winds), continue down this amazing valley until you reach **Phobjika valley**, a thriving potato growing centre. From November to April try to spot the rare **black-necked crane**. These large birds — usually a flock of some 200 — migrate from northern Tibet to Bhutan to winter here and in Bumdeling, just north of Tashiyangtse. The sight of the majestic birds flying over the fields and marshes of this undisturbed valley is truly memorable. Show the cranes the same respect that the Bhutanese do: don't shout or frighten them

If returning to Thimphu from Phobjika, the drive takes four hours so you can be back in Thimphu for dinner. For

Black-necked cranes

those heading eastwards, it is another three hours by road to Tongsa from the Phobjika turning.

The **Pele La pass** at 3,390m (11,121ft) crosses the lofty Black Mountains, the natural boundary between west and central Bhutan. From October to April you will encounter yaks enjoying the short high-altitude bamboo, and in spring, flowering rhododendron and magnolias. With luck, and good timing, you may be able to glimpse Jomolhari from the summit.

On the way down are two pretty villages, **Rukubji** and **Chendebji,** just across the river. The bird painted on a house near the bridge in **Nikkarchu** is the end point of the arduous Snowman Trek (see the chapter on *Trekking*). After 45 minutes from the top of the pass, the 18th-century **Chendebji Chorten** appears on the right. From here, the road to Tongsa is very dramatic as it cuts through the mountain with a fearsome 1,000m (3,300ft) drop. The road that is visible far across the valley winds south from Tongsa via Shemgang to Geleyphug on the Indian border.

For over 300 years, weary travellers have been impressed by the looming Tongsa Dzong, a splendid sight after a long and arduous journey across the valleys. The dzong's imposing size and extraordinary location denote the importance of the Tongsa Penlop, governor of central and east Bhutan, in the early days. From the chorten viewpoint, built in 1991, the dzong seems very close but it takes another half hour to get there.

Chendebji Chorten

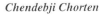

Central Bhutan

A trip to central Bhutan can be infinitely rewarding if you are mentally prepared to rough it out for a few days. More severe than the west, the landscape is dominated by dark forests and buckwheat fields. Central Bhutan is historically a deeply religious region. Dozens of small private temples and monasteries are hidden in the folds of the mountains, and the area is also the home of the splendid and unforgettable Tongsa Dzong.

A 4-wheel drive vehicle is recommended as the road is not very stable and prone to landslides in rain. Before you leave, remember to double check that the car is roadworthy and the spare tyre inflated. Take your own sleeping bag, if you prefer. A down jacket and woollen sweaters are necessary all year.

If you don't wish to linger in Punakha and Wangdiphodrang, a six-hour drive gets you direct to Tongsa from Thimphu over the Dochu La and Pele La passes. With a detour to Punakha Dzong (see *Itinerary 7*), the journey takes seven to eight hours.

Tongsa, the most impressive dzong in Bhutan

A stroll through Tongsa village and a visit to the 16th-century Tongsa Dzong.

Spend the night either at the relatively comfortable but expensive **Sherubling Lodge** just above Tongsa Dzong, or the more economical **Yangkhyll Hotel** in town. Despite basic rooms, the Yangkhyll's congenial kitchen is the only warm place in damp Tongsa. The lady of the house cooks well and makes you feel part of the family.

Around 8am stroll down the main street to **Tongsa Dzong**, which can be visited only with a permit. Tongsa Dzong was built at different periods on a spur overlooking the Mangde River. The intricacy of its maze of buildings on successive levels is clearly visible from the town. Beyond any doubt, the dzong's size, design and position make it the most impressive in Bhutan. First erected in 1543 by the Drukpa lama Ngagi Wangchuck, great grandfather of Shabdrung Ngawang Namgyel, the original building is found at the far end of the dzong, the Chorten Lhakhang.

In 1647, the Shabdrung Ngawang Namgyel, perceiving the strategic importance of the eastern road, built a fortress he called Choekhor Rabtentse Dzong. In 1652, it was enlarged by Minjur Tenpa, the third Temporal Ruler of Bhutan. More than a hundred years later, the **Maitreya Temple** and the section where the 200 monks live today were added.

After the 1897 earthquake, the dzong was repaired several times, notably by the first King Ugyen Wangchuck. It now contains 23 temples and a press where religious books are printed in the traditional form. The inside of **Chorten Lhakhang** is painted with beautiful images of the Buddha Mitrugpa (Akshobya) and contains the huge funeral chorten of lama Ngagi Wangchuck. The dzong is now the headquarters of the Tongsa district and houses the provincial monastic community. However, a large number of monks migrate to Kuje Lhakhang in Bumthang for the summer.

If you have time, go out through the small door on the right below the police post and then turn and walk back up the old narrow slippery path. The overwhelming mass of the dzong towering above makes you appreciate the feeling of might and power it gave to those arriving on foot in olden times.

After visiting Tongsa Dzong, return to town and walk up to **Ta Dzong**, the watchtower which overlooks it. Its architecture with two aisles protruding from the main building is unusual. The main temple, established in 1977, is dedicated to King Gesar, the deity and hero of the great Tibetan Buddhist epic. In the tale, the Warrior King Gesar of Ling is commissioned by Guru Rinpoche to vanquish the forces threatening the Dharma (Buddhist teachings).

If you still have time, look for curios in town, or settle down in the warm kitchen of the Yangkhyll, overlooking the dzong, to write letters or postcards.

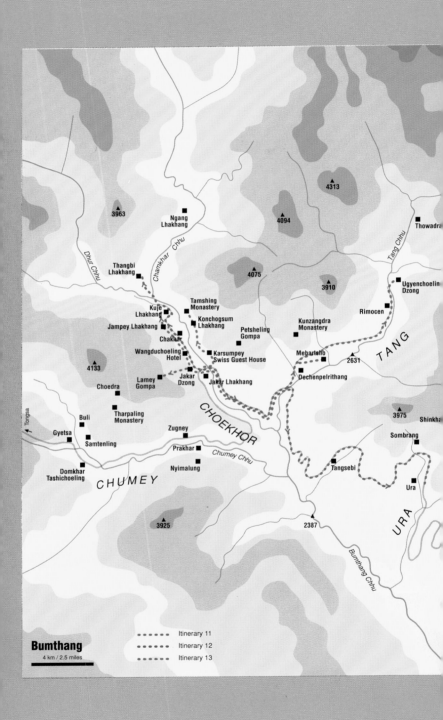

Bumthang
4 km / 2.5 miles

······· Itinerary 11
······· Itinerary 12
······· Itinerary 13

Leave for Jakar, the capital of Bumthang where you visit the 8th-century Wangduchoeling Palace.

It takes 2½ hours to drive to Jakar, the capital of Bumthang. Names are confusing because some Bhutanese speak of Bumthang, some of Jakar and some of Byakar.

Bumthang is the general name of the region which comprises the four valleys of Chume, Choekhor, Tang and Ura. Jakar refers exclusively to the Jakar Dzong, located in the Choekhor valley, which is the capital of the Bumthang region. Byakar is simply the Dzongkha spelling for Jakar but is pronounced the same.

Accommodation can be a problem in Bumthang so be sure to make bookings from Thimphu.

Ladies weaving yatra wool cloth

The **Wangduchoeling Hotel,** near the Wangduchoeling Palace is charming, with comfortable rooms and attached bathrooms with hot water. Though relatively expensive, it is good value for money. The dining room, with its lovely paintings, is a pleasant place to relax around the fire, though the food is overpriced. The **Swiss Guesthouse** at Karsumpey is smaller and more like a mountain hut with common showers, an outhouse down the garden and basic facilities. Forget about privacy but the guesthouse is convivial, economical, and has great food. For something in between in terms of price and facilities, try the **Tamshing Lodge** located on the way to Tamshing Monastery.

After leaving Tongsa, the road climbs quickly with good views of the Tongsa Dzong. It traverses a forest of rhododendrons and old decimated trees. After the **Yuto La pass** at 3,400m (11,155ft), the dramatic scenery changes to gentle spruce- and fir-covered slopes, reminiscent of the Swiss Alps. This is Bumthang, a scenic area speckled with numerous beautiful small temples and monasteries. The road then levels off into the wide **Chume valley** at 2,700m (8,860ft), and passes through a number of small villages.

After the Gyetsa hydro project, stop at the village of **Zugney** in Chume to watch ladies weaving *yatras*, the speciality of the region. These brightly coloured wool fabrics are usually displayed outside the houses. Quality, patterns and colour vary, and the ladies are tough and expert bargainers. After Zugney, do not miss the scenic village of **Prakar** on the right with its old mansion overlooking the river, belonging to the ancient lords of Chume.

After the **Kiki La** (2,900m/9,515ft), the **Choekhor valley** (2,600m/8,530ft) spreads before you with its backdrop of snowy

Jakar town

peaks. On the left towers the Jakar Dzong and straight ahead, at the valley's end, the Kuje Lhakhang complex. Some 8km (5 miles) later you arrive in **Jakar**, a tiny village.

You will be amazed by the proliferation of new houses and the air of relative prosperity in this area. Bumthang has changed tremendously in the last 10 years: time was when it took three days to travel from Thimphu. The construction of the new road, the provision of electricity, potato cultivation and improved animal husbandry have given a healthy boost to the economy of the region.

Upon arrival, visit the nearby **Wangduchoeling Palace** with its rows of prayer wheels. It was built in 1856 on an 8th-century site by the powerful Tongsa Penlop Jigme Namgyel, father of the first King Ugyen Wangchuck who was born here.

11. Bumthang

Visit Jampey Lhakhang, Kuje Lhakhang, Jakar Dzong and Lamey Gompa in the morning. The afternoon is spent at Konchogsum Lhakhang and Tamshing Monastery.

Leave around 8.30am if you have the relevant permits to visit the temples, 9am if not. Pass the hospital and head for **Jampey Lhakhang**, revered as one of the oldest temples in Bhutan. Like Kyichu in Paro (see *Itinerary 1*), Jampey Lhakhang is said to date back to the 7th century. To overcome the demoness who was occupying Tibet and threatening Buddhism, King Songtsengampo built this temple on her knee.

The shape of the structure today dates only from the beginning of the 20th century when three temples were built next to the original shrine. Surrounded by a circumambulation path, the temple contains a very holy image of Jampa (Maitreya), the Buddha of the Future after whom it is named.

Kuje Lhakhang, Bumthang

Across the fields from Jampey Lhakhang, the **Kuje Lhakhang** complex will undoubtedly catch your attention. Always a special place in Bhutan, the temple is associated with Guru Rinpoche. In the 8th century, Bumthang was ruled by King Sendha, who was at war with a king from the south. This rival killed Sendha's son and, in his extreme grief, Sendha forgot to worship his personal deity who took revenge by snatching the king's life force, causing him to fall mortally ill. Guru Rinpoche, because of his miraculous powers, was called to Bumthang to help King Sendha recover. He went to Kuje where the deity was residing and tricked it with a magical device. King Sendha recovered and Bumthang embraced Buddhism. In the rock where Guru Rinpoche meditated is the imprint of his body, which is what 'Kuje' means. The complex is now enclosed by a fence of small stone chortens, making it very sacred.

On entering, you see three temples and the funerary chortens dedicated to the three kings of Bhutan. Facing the temples, the first on the right is the oldest and contains the rock with Guru Rinpoche's body imprint. This building dates from 1652, during the time of Minjur Tenpa, the Tongsa Penlop. The second temple was built by Ugyen Wangchuck in 1900 when he was still Tongsa Penlop and houses a huge image of Guru Rinpoche, protector of Bhutan. In the porch outside the shrine, beautiful paintings depict protective and local deities. The third temple is built in traditional style and blends wonderfully with the older buildings, although it was

Jakar Dzong, or the Fortress of the White Bird

consecrated only in 1990 and is still not complete. Patronised by the Royal Family and especially by Ashi Kesang, the Queen Mother, it is a superb example of the high standard of current workmanship in Bhutan. Some say the stately cypress behind the temples grew from a walking staff used by Guru Rinpoche.

Return to Jakar and visit the **Jakar Dzong.** Also known as the Fortress of the White Bird, the dzong was founded in 1549 by the Drukpa lama Ngagi Wangchuck who built the fortress on the site where a white bird landed. It was enlarged in 1646 by the Shabdrung Ngawang Namgyel and restored in 1683 by Tenzin Rabgye, the fourth Temporal Ruler, who also added a tower and water tank. In 1897, the dzong was badly damaged by earthquake and was rebuilt in 1905 by Ugyen Wangchuck, apparently on a smaller scale. The headquarters of the Bumthang district is established here but there are no resident monks.

It is difficult to see the dzong at close quarters and it looks best from afar. Drive up past it to **Lamey Gompa**, a beautiful royal mansion dating from the 19th century. Formerly a royal monastery, it now houses a forestry office, and will soon be repaired and restored by the Swiss. Coming down the road, there is an excellent view of the dzong and water tower.

Village school

Lunch at your hotel or guesthouse as the restaurants in town are not very reliable. Beware of the afternoon wind which can blow hard and cold so take along warm clothes. Drive along the left bank of the river past the so-called **Swiss Farm**. This is the only good automobile workshop east of Thimphu so arrange to have your vehicle checked. You can also buy excellent cheese and locally-made schnapps for picnics.

About 3km (2 miles) on is a mansion on the other bank of the river below a cliff. This is **Chakhar**, the Iron Castle, the ancient residence of King Sendha and still inhabited by one of his descendants, the Chakhar Lama. Soon you reach a tiny fenced temple on the right side of the road, but do not be misled by its size. **Konchogsum Lhakhang** dates back to the 8th century. The inscription on a large bell testifies to it being cast for the Tibetan Royal Family, and the main image is that of the Buddha Namparnanzey (Vairocana). The pillar erected next to the entrance gate is said to be a megalith from prehistoric times.

Hardly a kilometre past Konchogsum is the lovely **Tamshing Monastery,** built between 1501 and 1505 by Pemalingpa, the great Bhutanese Nyingmapa lama (1450–1521). This private monastery contains some of the most remarkable paintings of this period in the Himalaya. Lining the circumambulation path on the ground floor of the monastery, and despite some damage, they constitute a unique documentation of Pemalingpa's teachings. The shrine, restored in the mid-20th century by the Royal Grandmother Ashi Phuntsho Choedron, is dedicated to Guru Rinpoche and his Eight Manifestations. Ask to see the coat of mail forged by Pemalingpa — it is believed that if you carry it thrice around the shrine your sins will be washed away.

The upper floor ceiling is low as Pemalingpa was said to have been very short in stature. An upper circumambulation path contains remarkable paintings, especially those related to the Three Bodies of the Buddha. Fine red drawings represent the Buddha of

Infinite Light, Oepamey (Amita-bha), Chenrezi, the Bodhisattva of Compassion (Avalokiteshwara) and Guru Rinpoche. The shrine is dedicated to the Buddha of Long Life, Tsepamey (Amitayus).

From Tamshing is an excellent view over Kuje Lhakhang, just the other side of the river. At Tamshing are cells for young monks who come to study and meditate. The place has a charming and peaceful atmosphere which has enchanted many.

Return to the Swiss Farm and the bridge across the river. Take the little footpath above the bridge leading to the temple and monastic school, Kharchhu She-drub Choeling. From here, the view over the dzong and the village is superb. Stroll back to the village. As in Tongsa, most of the shops are owned by Bhutanese of Tibetan origin. Have a look at the carpentry workshop at the foot of the hill of the dzong. You may be able to buy a nice, though cumbersome, Bhutanese table. In the evening arrange to eat *kule*, slightly bitter buck-wheat pancakes, or *buta*, buck-wheat noodles, both of which are the specialities of Bumthang. Both must be ordered ahead.

If the weather is fine, this itinerary, covering about 10km (6 miles), can be done on foot as Bumthang is quite flat. If you are staying at Wangduchoeling Hotel, turn right and walk past the hospital. Walk straight down the road to Jampey Lhakhang and Kuje Lhakhang, then cross the bridge and visit Tamshing, Konchogsum, the Swiss Farm, the bridge and Jakar village. Do it the other way round if you are staying at the Swiss Guesthouse.

Day Walks from Bumthang

If you have extra days and like walking, there are two treks from Bumthang that I would like to mention briefly. Unless you are a botanist or forester, these day walks are not recom-mended from early June to the end of September because of the rains.

Those who need to return can drive in one day from Bumthang to Thimphu. Leave no later than 8am with a stop for tea in Tongsa and a picnic break at Chendebji Chorten. It is an 8½-hour drive to the capital which will seem like a big metropolis! From the end of May until September, be sure to allow a full day between arriving back from Bumthang and your de-parture flight in case of delays caused by landslides.

Always go with a Bhutanese or someone who knows the way as you can easily get lost in the forest and the bears, plentiful in Bumthang, can be dangerous when surprised. Take a hat, flashlight, water-bottle, some food, a knife and a warm jacket.
• Trek through the forest to Lamey Gompa, up the old Kiki La Pass at 4,000m (13,000ft), see the Tharpaling Monastery (3,600m/11,800ft), and then drop down to Gyetsa/Domkhar on the road where the car should be waiting for you near the sawmill.
• Walk from the Swiss Farm up to Petseling Gompa and down to the Tang Valley via Kun-zangdra Monastery. Arrange for the car to meet you at the point where the Kunzangdra trail hits the road.

A leisurely morning walk to Thangbi Lhakhang. After lunch, take a drive to the Tang valley. Visit the Mebartsho holy site, Kunzangdra Monastery and Rimocen temple

Leave at 8.30am and drive a little beyond Kuje Lhakhang. Where the motorable road ends, start walking. The trail is quite wide and relatively flat and passes through forest. About 30 minutes later you will see a plateau to the right. At this point, leave the main trail and take the tiny path on the right down to a small creek. Cross the bridge and after a short climb you reach the plateau and see **Thangbi Lhakhang** in the distance, surrounded by farmhouses. Even without the permit to visit the temple, this is an easy two-hour walk through the beautiful upper Choekhor valley.

Thangbi Lhakhang was founded in 1470 by the fourth Shamar Rinpoche, an important lama of the Karma Kagyudpa sect. He left the region a few years later and Pemalingpa took over the temple, which then became a Nyingmapa place of worship. The iron curtain at the entrance is said to have been cast by the great saint himself. The temple's lower shrine is dedicated to the Buddhas of the Three Ages, and the upper sanctuary to the historical Buddha in the form of an eight-year-old prince.

Have an early lunch at your guesthouse then drive to the **Tang valley** at 2,800m (9,200ft). Turn right after the bridge at the end of the village and take the road east to Ura. Soon you reach the

Ugyenchoeling Dzong

southern part of the Tang valley. Leave the Dechenpelrithang Sheep Farm to the left and a kilometre on take the rough road up to the left. The holy site and pilgrimage place of **Mebartsho** is very close but take a guide with you as it is hard to know the spot from where you must walk for another five minutes. There is no temple but the site itself is sacred. Mebartsho means Burning Lake, but it is more of a gorge than a lake, and the name refers to the most famous episode of Pemalingpa's life. In early 1475, the saint discovered holy relics hidden here by Guru Rinpoche and thus received

Ponies are used by farmers

his holy mission to propagate religion. To silence sceptical minds, he plunged into the river with a burning lamp and declared: 'If I am a demon, I shall die! If I don't, and I am the true spiritual son of Guru Rinpoche, this lamp will continue to burn and I will recover hidden treasures!' Pemalingpa discovered the treasures, and the place took its present name.

If the road is good, drive further along the Tang valley, an agricultural region specialising in sheep rearing. At 3,350m (11,000ft) on a cliff opposite is **Kunzangdra Monastery**, founded by Pemalingpa in 1488. The hamlet of his birthplace, **Chel**, is not far. About 4km (2½ miles) on, after passing the primary school, you reach **Rimocen**. A huge rock overlooks this temple which marks one of Guru Rinpoche's meditation spots. It was established in the 14th century by the saint Dorjelingpa and restored in the mid-19th century by one of his descendants, the Tongsa Penlop Tshokye Dorje, whose own residence **Ugyenchoeling Dzong** overlooks the area, a 30-minute walk from the end of the road.

13. Ura Valley

A leisurely half-day excursion to the Ura valley, east of Bumthang.

If the weather is good leave at 9am with a packed lunch and drive to the **Ura valley** at 3,100m (19,200ft), the highest and most eastern of the Bumthang valleys. The journey takes about two hours from Jakar. Just before reaching the **Shelthang pass** at 3,600m (11,800ft), look back towards the north. In clear weather, you can see the huge white **Gangkar Punsum** (7,239m/23,750ft), the highest peak in Bhutan. It is a splendid sight but the mountain is visible only from a short strip of road, so don't miss it.

The landscape of Ura valley is characterised by broad sweeping slopes, clement pastures and wide fields. At the bottom is a large village with clusters of big houses linked by little alleys paved with stone slabs, a rare sight in Bhutan. Ura has enjoyed recent prosperity partly due to the cultivation of potatoes, and the villagers now compete at having the most opulent house. Leave the car and wander in the village, dominated by a temple consecrated in 1986 and dedicated to Guru Rinpoche. Have your picnic in Ura before returning to Jakar.

East Bhutan

A trip to the eastern part of the country offers only spartan and often difficult conditions but the rewards are commensurate – you will discover a Bhutan that is very different from the west and central areas.

The climate is milder with semi-tropical flora and fauna and the land is relatively densely populated with the Sharchopas, the easygoing, friendly and religious easterners. They speak a language called Tsangla, but more commonly known as Sharchopkha. There are very few open valleys (Radi and Tashiyangste being the most significant), rivers run through vertical gorges and most of the villages are perched along steep, often deforested, slopes. To give you an idea of the rugged terrain, climbs up and down of 1,000m (3,300ft) to cross a river are very common and you may have sev-

East Bhutan is a botanist's paradise

Buddhist monk

eral in a day's walk, although east Bhutan is generally at a lower altitude than the rest of the country. A visit is best from October to mid-May, although in winter, snow may delay you on the passes. The monsoon season from May to end September is to be avoided as roads may be closed for days because of landslides. The monsoon, which is heavier in the east, shrouds the country in clouds and brings out the leeches.

You will need a 4-wheel drive vehicle, and be prepared for lots of bumpy driving. Petrol is available in Bumthang, Mongar and Tashigang. Make sure that you always keep a spare tank of petrol in case of emergencies. There are mechanical workshops only in Bumthang and Mongar.

If you're returning to west Bhutan, you need 4 to 10 days to get to and from Bumthang. However, it is now possible to exit Bhutan through Assam with only an Indian visa, but keep in mind that this Indian state is still in political turmoil.

With only four days at your disposal, you have to give Lhuntse (see *Itinerary 15*) a miss and proceed directly to Tashigang (see *Itinerary 16*), returning to Mongar after a visit to Radi valley (see *Itinerary 17*). Those with time can include Tashiyangtse and Pemagatshel (see *Itineraries 18* and *19*). These suggestions can be shuffled to suit your schedule.

14. Bumthang to Mongar

Drive from Bumthang via Ura valley and across the Trumsing La pass to Mongar.

Today's drive is 141km (88 miles) and takes six hours. Leave your guesthouse around 8am with a packed lunch and arrive after two hours in the Ura valley where you can stop and visit the village and temple (see *Itinerary 13*). Have lunch in the meadows and then leave for Mongar. Drive up the road for one hour to the **Trumsing La pass** at 3,800m (12,500ft) through woodland. In May, you are likely to see yellow rhododendrons in bloom, a species not found at lower altitudes. The pass forms the boundary between central and east Bhutan and has beautiful views over the Himalaya if the weather is clear.

The next couple of hours will afford one of the most amazing driving experiences imaginable. You leave this cold high pass to find yourself two hours later at 650m (2,100ft) in semi-tropical forest! The dramatic plunge in altitude, with its extraordinary ecological contrasts, is truly impressive and must be one of the most impressive drives in the world. The narrow road cuts straight into the rocky mountain and winds through a series of hairpin curves with a deadly drop of hundreds of metres. Keep cool and drive slowly. Signboards with dubious humour warn: 'If You Like My Curves, I Have Many'. About 20km (12 miles) from the top of the

Mongar valley

pass, **Sengor** village huddles in a large meadow at 3,000m (10,000ft), a good place to stop for a picnic on the way back. The road continues to descend towards the semi-tropical zone, which starts around **Namning** at 2,200m (7,200ft), and where the landscape becomes softer and the weather warmer.

Lingmithang and **Kuri Zampa** are the lowest points on the road. At Kuri Zampa is a big Nepalese-style chorten and an interesting small factory that produces essential oils. East Bhutan, in common with French Provence, is rich in plants and herbs used in the perfume industry. The road crosses the River Kuri, flowing from the north, before it ascends again to 1,700m (5,500ft) cutting through a forest of chir pines and maize fields to **Mongar**.

In Mongar you have a choice between the **Shongar Lodge**, near the dzong, run by the Bhutan Tourism Corporation Limited, or the **Druk Kuenden Guesthouse**, located in town. Order food well in advance at the Druk Kuenden, as it can take some time to prepare. Mongar does not have much to offer in terms of restaurants but there are a few eating houses in the bazaar where the standard fare is rice, vegetables, lentils and omelette, and maybe noodle soup.

15. Lhuntse

Drive from Mongar to the northern district of Lhuntse. Visit the Lhuntse Dzong and spend the night.

Mongar has good weather and a pleasant setting but there is not much to see. The old main street shacks are slowly being replaced with beautiful stone houses. The **Mongar Dzong**, built in the 19th century and restored in 1953 and 1990, houses the district headquarters and monastic community. Leave around 10am for **Lhuntse**,

77km (48 miles) to the north. The journey can take up to four hours as the road is poor. Take food with you for lunch, not forgetting the delicious Bumthang cheese. The road to Lhuntse starts 12km (7½ miles) below Mongar off the road to Kuri Zampa.

The scenery is quite dramatic as you drive along the left bank of the Kurichu River gorge. It seems bereft of any human habitation as all the villages are hidden high up in the mountains. Next, you pass the two hamlets of **Aotsho** and **Gurgaon** where you may be able to get a plate of rice, some vegetables and tea.

After some 30km (19 miles) you reach **Thangmachu**, where you cross to the right bank of the river and continue upstream, still in the gorge at about 1,300m (4,265ft). The **Lhuntse Dzong** will suddenly appear, as if blocking the horizon. The road climbs steeply to the dzong at 1,700m (5,580ft) and only then do you realise that the valley extends far beyond and the dzong is built on the mountainside. Lhuntse Dzong (you need a permit for entry) was built in 1654 and has been restored many times. It houses about 100 monks and is the headquarters of the Lhuntse district, often called by its old name of Kurtoe. Lhuntse is a populated district and although officially belonging to east Bhutan, the northern part is culturally and linguistically more akin to Bumthang.

Lhuntse is famous for its girl-weavers who produce a brocade fabric called *kishutara*. The district also boasts numerous temples and places of historical interest such as Dungkar, where the present Royal Family hails, but these can be only be reached on foot.

The only place to stay is the **Government Guesthouse** and it is best to carry food with you as Lhuntse is still in the process of becoming a village. Spend the remainder of the afternoon exploring.

The next day leave Lhuntse by 7.30am to retrace your footsteps to Mongar in time for an early lunch. If you have the energy, make the worthwhile detour to Dametsi (see *Itinerary 16*). If you go direct, it is only 2½ hours drive between Mongar and Tashigang so you could leave Lhuntse a little later in the morning.

Musicians at a religious festival

Travel overland from Mongar to Tashigang with a detour to the Dametsi Monastery.

After having had a quick look around Mongar town, leave around 10am with a packed lunch for Tashigang, 2½ hours and 96km (60 miles) to the east. If you can afford the time, do not miss the detour to Dametsi and plan to eat your picnic lunch there. The round trip back to the main road adds 3½ hours, making the excursion a total of six hours. The road climbs from Mongar to the **Kori La pass** at 2,298m (7,539ft) through forests of oak and fern before dropping past the **Nagtshang Temple** to the village of **Yadi**. The famous Yadi Zigs are an impressive 20-km (12-mile) stretch of relentless curves.

The bottom of the mountain is reached when you cross the Sherichu River at 700m (2,300ft). From here, the route is straight and relatively flat until almost Tashigang. The road follows the Gamrichu, one of the main rivers of Bhutan and a tributary of the Brahmaputra that eventually becomes the Manas River in India.

Some 13km (8 miles) after crossing the Sherichu River, branch left and drive north for about 20km (12 miles) to the site of the wonderful **Dametsi Monastery**. The largest monastery in east Bhutan, Dametsi is an important place, built in the 16th century by a descendant of the great Nyingma saint Pemalingpa. Rebuilt as a dzong in the 17th century, it has been restored many times, most recently in 1990. There is also a lovely village situated on a plateau at 2,400m (7,900ft) with a good view over east Bhutan — the Tashigang region and the high Himalayan peaks to the left and the plateau of Kanglung straight ahead with the buildings of Sherubtse College and the distant Bromsing La.

Tashigang Dzong

Brokpas in Tashigang

Back on the main road it is only a 45-minute drive to Tashigang along the Gamrichu gorge. Of the town you can see nothing except the dzong, perched high on a buttress above the Chazam Bridge, which is amply adorned with prayer flags. Have your permit ready for a police checkpost after the bridge.

The road ascends to the charming little town of **Tashigang** at 1,150m (3,773ft). Headquarters of the most thickly populated district in Bhutan with 150,000 people, the town shelters about 2,000 inhabitants. It is built along a slope forming a small half-circle behind the spur on which stands the Tashigang Dzong. The temperature is pleasantly cool in winter but hot in summer. Poinsettia and bougainvillaea thrive in this region as do banana, orange and papaya trees.

The only place to stay in Tashigang is the **Kelling Lodge**, so book well in advance. Situated beyond the centre of the town and the hospital, each room, though simple, has an attached bathroom with hot water when there is electricity.

After settling in, return on foot to the town and enjoy the relaxing atmosphere of Tashigang. Many of the well-stocked shops and small restaurants have pleasant outside seating areas from where you may watch the world go by. Activity centres on the open square which doubles as the bus station. In winter, you will see the Brokpas, the people from the isolated valley of Sakteng. The Brokpas are easily recognised by their round black hats made of yak-hair and distinctive clothes sewn from coarse red wool and animal skins.

The food is fine at the Kelling Lodge but you are encouraged to try the local restaurants such as the **Puensum** near the bus station, recommended for its meat. The food will be generally the same everywhere. Stop by for a drink in the **Norkhyil Bar** in the lower market, a favourite with well-to-do locals. The **bakery** opposite makes excellent Tibetan bread every morning, a great improvement on the usual tasteless factory-made bread.

A brief visit to scenic Radi valley. Return to Tashigang in the afternoon to visit its distinctive dzong.

Leave at 8am from Tashigang for the round trip to Radi which takes about 3½ hrs and is interesting for its scenery and the superb view of Tashigang Dzong. The road to Radi branches left just after the main market, below a cement arch. After a few hundred metres, look back at Tashigang Dzong which majestically overshadows the Gamrichu gorge. Turn right or eastwards, and follow the narrow Gamrichu valley at about 900m (3,000ft) above sea level. About 10km (6 miles) further, past the shops of **Lungten Zampa**, the rough road starts climbing and after 14km (9 miles) reaches the idyllic **Radi valley** at 1,600m (5,250ft). Before Radi village proper, you will come to Rangjung, where a new monastery and religious school, Rangjung Woesel Choeling, is under construction.

A large valley by east Bhutan standards, Radi produces excellent rice, an uncommon crop in these parts where maize is ubiquitous. The farmhouses are scattered among the paddy fields and surrounded with banana and orange trees. You may be able to watch local women weaving the superb raw silk fabric called *menzimatra* or *lungserma*.

Head back around noon and visit **Tashigang Dzong** which peculiarly has only one courtyard. Built from 1656–1659 by the Drukpas after their conquest of east Bhutan, the dzong has an important strategic position and today houses the district administration and monastic community. Remember that you'll need a special permit to enter.

Plan to be back for lunch at 1pm in town so that you can pack your bag and leave around 3pm, giving you sufficient time to be back in Mongar before dark.

Yak ploughing at Radi valley

18. Tashiyangtse

A day trip to Tashiyangtse, famous for its dzong and the Nepalese-style Chorten Kora Stupa, site of an annual festival.

Start at 9am and carry food and drink for today's journey. Turn right after crossing the Chazam Bridge; you are now heading upstream on the right bank of first the Gamrichu and then the Bamrichu rivers. The altitude is barely 750m (2,500ft) and the mountains tower above the road. Only 24km (15 miles) from Tashigang is **Gom Kora** where to the right a temple stands on terraced rice fields above the river. Near it a huge black rock marks the holy place where Guru Rinpoche is said to have subdued a demon. An important festival is held here in March or April each year.

Soon after Gom Kora you reach **Doksum**, a small village at the head of two valleys where women can be seen weaving outside their homes. The right-hand valley has no road and runs east to India, whilst the one on the left leads north to Tashiyangtse and Chorten Kora.

Slowly ascend the left bank of the Kulongchu River and enter a forested region where you may see

Chorten Kora

monkeys. Some 20km (12 miles) after Doksum, the small **Tashiyangtse Dzong** (1,850m/6,070ft) appears on a hillock across the river. Built in 1656, the dzong was renovated in 1976, and since Tashiyangtse became a separate district in 1993, has housed the District Administration. Walk down to the old bamboo and cane bridge, a beautiful example of Bhutanese craftsmanship.

Driving on another 5km (3 miles), the gorge abruptly opens into a wide valley of rice fields. In the middle is the impressive **Chorten Kora**, whose setting makes the whole trip worthwhile. This whitewashed chorten is the largest in Bhutan and the scene of a festival in February or March each year when ceremonies are performed by monks from the nearby temple. Built in 1782, it was restored in the 20th century. Next to the chorten, do not miss an interesting interpretation of the Wheel of Life painted under an archway.

For a good picnic spot, go through the village to the lovely meadow near the cement bridge. After lunch, cross the bridge and walk for an hour or two up the quiet and peaceful valley. A full 2½-hour walk north of Tashiyangtse will bring you to the valley of Bumdeling, where a flock of some 160 black-necked cranes come to winter between November and April each year.

Drive 55km (34 miles) back to Tashigang, which will take about two hours, and enjoy an evening in town.

Onward to Kanglung, site of Bhutan's only college; a scenic drive past Yongphu La pass; Khaling with its Blind School and Weaving Centre; and on to Pemagatshel for the night.

Leave Tashigang at 8am and take the road south past the petrol pumps. The road climbs steadily for 45 minutes to the plateau of Kanglung, winding through lovely inhabited areas such as Pham and Rongthong. **Kanglung** at 2,200m (7,220ft) is famous throughout the country as the site of Bhutan's only college. **Sherubtse College**, meaning the Peak of Knowledge, was established in 1978 and has more than 500 students of the arts, commerce and sciences. Currently affliated to New Delhi University in India, the college aims to become an autonomous university with courses in Bhutanese history, language and environmental sciences. Students stroll in the pleasant, sprawling campus carrying their books or going for a bite at **Phala's**, an excellent restaurant found at the ground floor of the two-storied building before the college gate. Stop here for tea after visiting the **Zangdopelri Temple,** opposite the college gate. Founded in 1978 and dedicated to Guru Rinpoche, the temple has lovely paintings.

From Kanglung the road climbs after 5km (3 miles) to the **Yongphu La pass** at 2,500m (8,200ft). Way across on the other side of the valley is Dametsi Plateau and the Yadi Zigs. This vantage point allows you to appreciate the complicated topography and deep valleys of east Bhutan. If you are lucky enough to have a cloudless day, the view over east Bhutan will be stunningly beautiful for the next hour covering the 32km (20 miles) to **Khaling**. This village nestles in the curve of a mountain at 2,200m (7,220ft), boasting an amazing Blind School and an interesting Weaving Centre. At the **Blind School,** you cannot fail to be touched by the dedication of

The Weaving Centre at Khaling

A flowered kira on the loom

the staff and the precociousness of the children who sometimes put up a little concert for their guests. The **Weaving Centre** is outside the village and sells fabrics and jackets in wonderful colour tones.

Have lunch in one of the restaurants in Khaling but do not expect great food. You will most probably see *Brokpas*, people from the remote high valley of Merak. Brokpas often migrate to this clement area to escape from the cold winter.

Leave Khaling not later than 2pm for Pemagatshel, a three-hour drive away. Along the way, stop at the village of **Wamrong**, an hour's drive away. In the winter months, you will see Brokpa women with their herds of sheep grazing among Daphne and Edgeworthia bushes. These plants are used to make the handmade paper that Bhutan is well-known for. There is a police check post just after Wamrong and a big hospital with lovely views at **Rizerboo** on the edge of a hill. The road to Pemagatshel branches off 20km (12 miles) later at **Tselingor**, a point marked only with a shack and rickety signboard, so take care not to miss it.

From Tselingor, leave the sweeping views of the high Himalaya and plunge down a bumpy road for the next 25km (16 miles) through thick semi-tropical forest. Perched high, like an eagle's nest, is the monastery of Yongle Gompa (see *Itinerary 20*). Along the way, you may also meet trucks carrying gypsum from Pemagatshel to the Indian border.

Pemagatshel is a small but well populated district built in the late 1970s. The village and its dzong are new but a number of historical temples and places of interest are scattered in the countryside. The town is built on a hillside overlooking a verdant tableau. The **Government Guesthouse**, behind the dzong, is small and basic. It has no restaurant facilities so you have to eat in one of the simple village restaurants. In ancient times Pemagatshel was one of only four routes into Bhutan.

Explore the town sights; Pemagatshel temple; Pemagatshel dzong; the Weaving Centre; and Yongle Gompa.

This morning leave your car at the guesthouse and start walking at about 8am. If it's a Sunday, have breakfast in the village and then wander round the little weekly market in front of the temple. Villagers sell vegetables and tuberous roots from the forest that you will not see elsewhere in Bhutan. The **Pemagatshel Temple** belongs to the Nyingmapa sect and the main statue represents Guru Rinpoche. Have a look at **Pemagatshel Dzong** before going down to the new **Weaving Centre** where young girls produce beautiful traditional fabrics, though they are not for sale. Have lunch in the village, then collect your car from the guesthouse.

Drive back down the road on which you arrived yesterday. About 5km (3 miles) from Kheri Gompa village, in a forest clear-

Street-seller in Pemagatshel

ing on the right, you will see prayer flags and a small pathway leading to Yongle Gompa. Park the car and start walking. The one-hour climb is not difficult and the trail goes through thick forest that some might find daunting, and others, very romantic. Unexpectedly, the forest clears and you reach a high point decorated with prayer flags and then a chorten. About 100m (330ft) away is the **Yongle Gompa**. Founded in the 16th century, Yongle Gompa is now a private Nyingmapa monastery headed by the eminent and respected Dodrupchen Rinpoche. The main statue represents Guru Rinpoche. On a clear day, the view from the monastery is one of the most breathtaking in all my years of trekking in the Himalaya. If you have binoculars, don't forget them today. You feel on top of the world, although you are only 2,350m (7,710ft) high. The panorama will have you feeling as if you're standing in the middle of a gigantic relief map: no nature lover can remain unmoved.

The Himalaya will stretch below you from Gangkar Punsum to Trumsing La, the pass separating central from east Bhutan, then Yadi, Dametsi and Tashigang. At your feet are Pemagatshel and the mountains of Merak Sakteng, and away to the south the green forested hills of Bhutan extend to the plateau of Deothang and the immensity of the Indian Plains.

Stay overnight at the guesthouse in Pemagatshel as the next morning you have to leave early for the seven-hour drive back to Mongar, with lunch in Tashigang.

If the weather is not clear in Pemagatshel, the excursion to Yongle Gompa is not worth the trip, unless you are a particularly religious person. Therefore an option which also saves a day is to return from Pemagatshel to Tashigang this afternoon and spend the night there. The next day's journey from Tashigang to Bumthang will take about 8½ hours of driving. If you are exiting through Samdrup Jongkhar, the journey from Tselingor takes about three hours. In sprawling Samdrup Jongkhar, with its unmarked Indo-Bhutan border, the best place to stay is the Jigten Hotel.

Approximate Driving Times between Major Bhutanese Towns

Phuntsholing to Paro/Thimphu	6 hrs
Paro to Thimphu	1½ hrs
Thimphu to Punakha/Wangdiphodrang	2 hrs
Thimphu to Tongsa	6 hrs
Tongsa to Bumthang	2½ hrs
Bumthang to Mongar	6 hrs
Mongar to Lhuntse	4 hrs
Mongar to Tashigang	2½ hrs
Tashigang to Tashiyangtse	2 hrs
Tashigang to Samdrup Jongkhar	6 hrs

TREKKING

Trekking in Bhutan presents a number of unique conditions, making it unsuitable for the individual traveller. Food and accommodation are scarce due to the sparse and isolated settlements. Trekking trails are neither obvious nor marked and there are no maps, so you can easily get lost in the forests. You will not know where to find water and wood or where to camp safely at night. All the food and equipment has to be carried yourself as porters and horses are not available for foreigners. In the light of these considerations, it is wise to leave individual trekking to countries like Nepal and book your Bhutan trek through a travel agent.

East Bhutan is seldom visited by trekkers

Bhutanese tour operators can organise trekking for foreigners visiting Bhutan on their own. A flat rate is charged per day and everything is provided. You need only bring along a sleeping bag and personal items. Trekking is also organised by international tour operators who specialise in tours to Bhutan. For those with limited time, this is definitely the recommended option. Heed advice as to the best routes for the time and season that you wish to visit.

Trekking in Bhutan offers both spectacular scenery and the chance to see villagers at work and play. Overall, the best time to trek in Bhutan is October, but the extreme variety of altitudes and climates makes it hard to generalise. April and May are also good but at higher altitudes you may still encounter snow and hail, and the occasional pre-monsoon shower lower down. November and March are fine for mid-level treks up to 3,000m (10,000ft). Early May to October is good for those wishing to go above 3,500m (11,500ft) but be prepared for some snow and rain. The end of June and July should be avoided because of the monsoon. If you are a botany buff, choose April and May for the rhododendrons, and August and September when alpine flowers are in bloom.

Whilst walking in Bhutan always be aware of the possibility of

mountain sickness. Treks start at 2,300m (7,550ft) and often go over 4,000m (13,000ft), depending on the route. Mountain sickness may affect anyone, regardless of age and fitness. It can be avoided by careful acclimatisation. Do not go too high too fast. Drink plenty of liquids to help your body adjust. Persistent headaches that do not recede with mild painkillers, disorientation, nausea or sleeplessness mean that you must rest. Descend if symptoms persist. If unheeded, mountain sickness can develop into potentially fatal cerebral or pulmonary oedema. Possibilities of medical evacuation are slim in Bhutan because there are no facilities for mountain rescue.

When trekking, keep Bhutan clean and green. Bhutan's mountain trails are still unpolluted and pristine as few trekkers use them. Please keep the trails that way. Respect the local people and their way of life and keep in mind that Bhutan is not a living museum for the pleasure of a few lucky foreigners, but a country struggling to improve its standard of living while striving to maintain a balance between progress and tradition.

Trekking routes vary in terms of time, difficulty and your personal interest. Ask your tour operator for more details.

Druk Path Trek goes in 3 or 4 days from Thimphu to Paro via Phajoding Monastery and surrounding lakes at 4,000m (13,000ft). It is relatively easy with excellent views of the Himalaya if the weather is clear. The rhododendrons are superb in April and May.

Bumthang Trek is an excellent 4–5 day introductory trek with beautiful scenery, rural villages and a pass at 3,400m (11,100ft). A good trek for April–May and October–November.

Gantey Gompa Trek is a highly recommended 3-day route for first-time trekkers and flower lovers. Especially spectacular in April when the rhododendrons and magnolias are in bloom.

Yak herdsmen

Samtengang Trek is an ideal 3-day walk for the winter months from November to February, passing through relatively low altitude (1,500–2,000m/5,000–6,500ft). Lookout for interesting villages along the way.

Jomolhari Trek takes you, in 7 days, to Jomolhari Base Camp in the beautiful region of Lingshi, country of yak herders, alpine vegetation and 4,900-m (16,000-ft) mountain passes. This route offers some of the most breathtaking close-up views of the great Himalayan peaks. Recommended for experienced trekkers. The best time is late September to October.

Laya Trek is a 7-day itinerary which ascends in easy stages to the village of Laya (4,000m/13,000ft), the home of some unique yak herders. This excellent trek, which takes you from semi-tropical

Women from Laya

forests to alpine pastures, includes visits to interesting villages and the Gasa Dzong, and boasts superb views of Masang Gang at 7,194m (23,602ft). The best time is October. When combined with the 14-day **Lingshi Trek**, it becomes more demanding and is recommended for tougher trekkers.

Lunana Trek, 18 days, is reserved for the hardy and adventurous and is rated as one of the most difficult and demanding. The only feasible time to attempt it is September, but even then early snow may be a problem. Initially following Lunana Trek, The **Snowman Trek** is the toughest trek in Bhutan: for 22 days, a real adventure taking you from 2,800m/9,186ft to 5,500m/18,000ft covering about 20km (12½ miles) a day, and traversing no less than 10 high passes. Note that these last four treks all pass through the Jigme Dorji National Park, Bhutan's largest protected forest area. Keep an eye out for interesting animals like the blue sheep, takin, pheasants, and, if you're lucky, the very elusive snow leopard.

Sakteng Trek takes you in an easy 5 days from Radi (1,700m/5,570ft) to Sakteng (3,000m/10,000ft), the easternmost valley in Bhutan. It becomes more demanding when extended by 2 days to **Merak** as a 4,200-m(13,800-ft) pass links the two valleys. Both Sakteng and Merak have a population of unusual yak herders and it is wonderful to see their way of life. Good in October and November with March and April being great for rhododendrons.

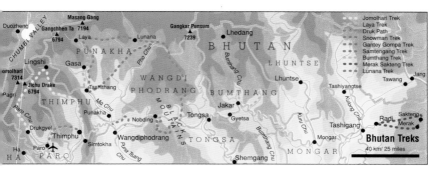

Bhutan Treks
40 km / 25 miles

- - - Jomolhari Trek
- - - Laya Trek
- - - Druk Path
- - - Snowman Trek
- - - Gantey Gompa Trek
- - - Samtengang Trek
- - - Bumthang Trek
- - - Merak Sakteng Trek
- - - Lunana Trek

Shopping

When shopping in Bhutan, forget about tourist trinkets or cute souvenirs, although you may find some imported from India and Nepal. Bhutan sells authentic objects, most of which are not geared towards the tourist trade. The artefacts you will find are mainly used in the daily life of the Bhutanese and are produced by the people for their own use.

Cottage-industry production is an area that is being actively promoted by the government, especially the National Women's Association. Remember that very little is made in factories so chances are that most of the items being sold are handmade and may have taken months of painstaking work. Many visitors find it a great pleasure to find items and crafts made with techniques now lost in many parts of the world. Because of the high demand for these handicrafts from the local community, supply rarely meets demand, resulting in relatively high prices compared with artefacts from neighbouring Nepal and India.

Bumthang yatra

An important cultural oddity to bear in mind when shopping is that the Bhutanese, for various complex reasons, tend to disdain people who bargain hard for their buys. You will find that Bhutan's shopkeepers are surprisingly unforthcoming and reticent. You can enter a shop, look around and leave without warranting so much as a glance from the proprietor. If you want something, you will have to ask for it. However, you will always be welcome, even if you do not buy anything. For serious shoppers though, this apparent lack of interest does not always augur well.

Although Thimphu has the widest selection of artefacts to be found this should not deter you from shopping in the other districts. In fact, some regions in the country have longer traditions than other places for certain types of crafts and, as a result, local workers and artisans tend to be more skilled than their counterparts elsewhere in Bhutan. Besides, prices can be more reasonable in the countryside and the money from your purchase goes directly to the artisans, or, at the least, remains in the community where the handicraft is produced.

As a general guide to the best buys, the best wool weavings come from Bumthang; intricate gold and silver ornaments are made in Paro and Thimphu; the most aesthetic and prized wooden bowls are carved in Tashiyangtse; the Kangpara valley in Tashigang, and Zhemgang district are famous for their bamboo and cane products; the finest silk and cotton textile weavings originate in the Lhuentse district.

Silk brocade

Handmade Fabrics

Bhutan's handmade fabrics are exquisite, ranging from US$15 to US$2,000, depending on whether you want simple cottons or heavy silk brocades which have taken over a year of laborious work. *Khaling* fabrics are less expensive and very attractive. Handwoven fabrics are usually sold as *kira* or dress piece. You can also buy table mats, purses, belts, jackets and a few other western-style items in Thimphu. Raw silk, or *bura*, used in men's ceremonial scarves, is ideal for shawls or tailored into blouses. Machine-woven Bhutanese cloth makes great outdoor shirts and is available at **Gyaltsen (Sephu) Tshongkhang**. Do not miss buying the twill-wool rolls called *yatras* which can be made into jackets or carpets. Prices range from US$60 to US$80, and even American designer Calvin Klein uses them in his international *haute couture* collections.

Wooden Bowls

Wooden bowls, often lacquered inside, are washable and used as eating utensils. Prices range from US$3 for a small drinking cup to US$40 for a larger container, according to the type and quality of wood used, although these distinctions are not always evident to outsiders. Silver-lined cups are more expensive.

Jewellery

Bhutanese jewellery is difficult to wear because of their weight. The best items, the large silver brooches which fasten the *kira*, range from US$40 to US$400, especially if they still have the chain which links them. Silver bracelets are interesting if you like heavy jewellery, but there are hardly any traditional rings or earrings left to sell. If you want to splurge, buy a carved betel nut silver box for about US$100.

Handmade Paper

Bhutanese paper is handmade from the bark of the Daphne and Edgeworthia shrub, and comes in rough sheets in a variety of colours. It makes for original wrapping paper and is a good writing base for calligraphy.

Bambooware

Bhutan is known for its handmade bamboo work, so famous that they were prized exports to Tibet in former times. Small round baskets known as *banchung*, 'Bhutanese Tupperware', are good buys, with prices starting from US$1.50.

Thangkas

Religious paintings called *thangkas,*

Shopping for *Thangkas*

Much sought after and rare, and often expensive in the West, a good *thangka* from Bhutan can be a sound investment, while, at the same time, yielding spiritual calm and pleasure.

Thangka painting is a painstaking art form and some of the better specimens, known as *lothangs*, can take up to a year to complete. The most respected artists employ the beautiful *kamthang*, or 'dry shading technique'.

However, many commercial artists today have learned to speed up the process by using flawed techniques that may not be obvious to the untrained eye. Here's how to tell an exceptional *thangka* from the generic, marketplace variety:

Hold the *thangka* with the painted side facing the sun or a strong artificial light. If you see rough, uneven shades of dark and light paint you are holding a fairly commonplace *thangka*. But if the background is a uniform shade, or the gradations between dark and light appear smoothly layered, chances are that it is the work of a highly skilled and patient artist. Of course, Buddhist humility dictates that all paintings remain unsigned.

Rule of thumb: Light, subtle treatment of the subject suggests more time and skill than thick strong colors. Prices for originals range from US$65 upwards.

Bamboo boxes

made from combinations of over 30 natural ingredients, are not cloying and sweet but deep, woodsy and refreshing. Buy some as unique reminders of your visits to the temples of Bhutan. Prices range from US$0.50 to US$2.00 a bundle.

Where to Shop in Thimphu

The best place to shop in Bhutan is Thimphu, although you may chance upon interesting items in smaller towns like Bumthang and Tashigang. There are now too many handicraft places in Thimphu to list. The following is only a general guide to give you an idea of what is available in town. Do not hesitate to explore the smaller shops for incense, Darjeeling tea, bricks and cones of tea, hard cheese cubes, Szechuan pepper, Bhutanese jackets and blouses and other memorabilia.

Handicrafts Emporium (just north of the bank on Norzim Lam), is best for basket work, traditional woven and *Khaling* fabrics, wooden artefacts, jewellery, masks, *thangkas*, and Bhutanese paper.

Ethometho, in the building next to the Cinema Hall, carries wooden artefacts, fabrics, postcards, posters, Bhutanese music cassettes and T-shirts.

The **ICDP Showroom**, on Chang Lam facing Changlimithang Stadium, has a selection of western style clothes made from traditional Bhutanese fabrics.

The Government Handicrafts Emporium for a good range of *thangkas*, bamboo crafts, jewellery, books and textiles.

Druk-Trin Rural Handicrafts, above the Sakten Health Club on Gatoen Lam, sells fabrics, baskets, and jewellery.

Choeki Handicrafts, below the Painting School, is very good for wooden artefacts and *thangkas*.

Tshering Drolkar, opposite the Cinema Hall and the Ethometho Building on Norzim Lam, is best for jewellery.

The **Weekend Market**, near the river, for wooden artefacts, cloth made out of yak-hair, and religious items.

Mangala and Jungshi Handmade Paper Factories are situated close together, behind Riverview Hotel.

•**Deejo Tshongkhang**, a few shops north of Hotel Kelwang on Norzim Lam, has religious statues and calendars.

which are faithful to the traditional iconography and done on cotton cloth, make wonderful gifts. Especially good are those painted with mineral and vegetable pigments. They are priced from US$20 for a simple unframed painting to US$200 for an elaborate subject framed in Chinese brocade. Antique *thangkas*, like the ones seen in the temples and monasteries, are not available for sale.

Masks

Colourful masks, like those used during religious dances, are made of papier-mache, seldom of wood. You can also find miniature masks of lesser quality but that are easier to pack in a suitcase.

Carpets

The Bhutanese used to import carpets from Tibet, and you can still find old Tibetan and Chinese carpets in Thimphu. Bhutanese-made modern carpets are factory-made and not of good quality.

Incense

Incense making evolved as an art in Bhutan from the traditional practice of producing rare herbs and essences. In ancient times, Bhutan was known as *Menjong*, Land of Medicinal Herbs. Based on formulas taught by leading spiritual masters and physicians and passed down from one generation to the next, these preparations are used not only as devotional offerings but also to relieve stress and induce a sense of calm. The fragrances,

Eating Out

Bhutan is not a place for fancy dining. The choice of ingredients is very limited and there are no restaurants as such except in Thimphu and Phuntsholing, where the tourist hotels offer a choice of Bhutanese, Indian, Chinese and Continental food. In the rest of country, eating houses offer a diet of rice and vegetable curry, and occasionally meat and eggs. The food in the small roadside restaurants is usually Indian-Bhutanese and quite different from the typical Bhutanese food cooked at home. Restaurants close early and orders are seldom accepted after 9pm. Always ask what is available that day as supplies can be erratic.

Food in Bhutan is best in private houses and is generally very hot. *Emadatsi*, or chilli peppers in cheese sauce, is the national dish. The reddish Bhutanese rice is usually accompanied by two or three dishes, all amply spiced with chillies. Meat is difficult to come by; yak meat is eaten fresh from October to December and dried the rest of the year. Vegetables are often cooked in a cheese sauce. Seasonal specialities include fresh chantarelle and shitake mushrooms, fiddlehead ferns, asparagus and even orchids and strange plants from the forest. Tibetan dishes such as steamed or fried *momos* (meat or cheese dumplings), *thukpa* (noodle soup) and *shabalay* (meat patties) are popular. Desserts are non-existent but some restaurants may offer tinned fruit salad, creme caramel and chocolate mousse. Fruit is eaten between meals.

Tea is the most popular drink, usually served Indian-style with milk and sugar. If you want it black, ask for *pika*. Traditional salt butter tea is served to foreigners only on special occasions and tastes better if thought of as a soup rather than tea. Coffee (or rather instant Nescafe) is more expensive and not as common as tea. Other options are Bhutanese-made canned fruit juices, and Indian-made soft drinks and mineral water. Foreign drinks are difficult to find so bring your favourite brand. Bhutanese whisky (Special Courier and Royal Supreme Whiskey) and fruit brandy are comparable to schnapps. Indian beer is widely available; Eagle, Black Label and Dansberg brands are the most popular.

While ordering meals in restaurants, provide clear, specific instructions, especially if you are a strict vegetarian. Otherwise you could well find the 'vegetarian' noodle soup you requested may not have solid meat but was really made with beef or chicken stock! Almost all Bhutanese people are meat eaters and locals can sometimes be too casual about special dietary preferences of other people, though never from malice.

Bhutanese food is usually prepared from natural ingredients but if you are ordering Indian, Chinese or Western dishes, the food almost invariably contains some Monosodium Glutamate (MSG), an artificial flavour enhancer

Family eating Bhutanese style

known here by their brand names Aji-nomoto and Weeching. If you are allergic to MSG (many people complain of an excessive dryness of mouth or tightness), inform the restaurant manager beforehand that you prefer your food MSG-free. Note: you might have more success being understood if you say Weeching or Aji-nomoto instead of MSG.

Restaurants in Thimphu

Hotel 89 at Chorten Lam serves Indian, Bhutanese, Chinese and Continental food in a warm, wood-panelled room. Open daily 7am–10pm. At **Plum's Cafe**, a bright place overlooking the main traffic roundabout on Norzim Lam, you will find Bhutanese, Chinese and Thai-inspired dishes, plus ribs, chicken wings and burgers. Try their deserts, but especially good is Plum's fabulous apple pie. Open daily 11am–10.30pm.

For more luxurious surroundings try **Hotel Riverview**, across Changlimithang Stadium, serving chic *hors d'oeuvres* (try their mushroom-stuffed tomatoes) with a range of soups and salads as well as other dishes. Open daily 8am–10pm. **Hotel Kelwang**, at Norzim Lam, across from the Druk Sherig Hotel, has an extensive menu with very good Indian, as well Bhutanese, Chinese and Continental dishes. Open daily, breakfast 7–10am, lunch noon–3pm and dinner 6–10pm. For Chinese, Bhutanese and Continental food in an elegant setting, head for **Hotel Taktsang**. The marble beneath your feet comes from the Gidakom valley south of Thimphu. Open daily for breakfast, lunch and dinner.

Consistently the best in town with good service to boot, the restaurant at **Hotel Druk** serves Bhutanese, Chinese, Continental, and excellent Indian dishes. Open daily for breakfast, lunch and dinner. **Jomolhari** serves Indian food, plus the usual Bhutanese, Chinese and Continental dishes. Open daily for breakfast, lunch and dinner. The **Swiss Bakery**, located above the traffic roundabout on Norzim Lam and serving sandwiches and pastries, is a popular lunch place. Open Monday to Saturday 8am–7pm. **Jichu Drakey Bakery**, off Chorten Lam, has

take-out chicken pastries, apple strudel, eclairs and croissants, or enjoy them there with coffee or tea in the small tearoom. Open daily 7am–noon, 1.30–7pm. At **Benez**, a small joint popular with the younger crowd, the pork *momos* and *thukpa* are especially good. Open daily 9.30am–10pm. **Sambara** at Gatoen Lam has good Chinese food and a bar. Open daily 10am–11pm.

The **Yeedzin Restaurant**, adjoining Jichu Drakey Bakery, is spacious and tastefully decorated with beautiful samples of Bhutanese textiles, the work of this establishment's in-house weavers, whom you may like to meet following a meal. The restaurant specialises in group orders for authentic Bhutanese cuisine. Open daily 7am–11pm.

Hotel City Centre, near Town Clock Tower, is the only place in town that has banned the use of MSG in their kitchen. Their 'honey-pork' dish features ham slices simmered in a delicate sauce of honey and garnished with spinach, spring onions and tomatoes. Open daily 8am–10pm.

Lhanam's, located around the corner from the Norzim Lam roundabout, serves a menu of Bhutanese, Indian and Chinese dishes. Immensely popular with young expatriate volunteers working in Bhutan. Open daily 9.30am–10pm, except on the last Sunday of the month.

Wangdi Restaurant is another recommendation, located a few paces short of the Norzim Lam roundabout. Despite its somewhat dingy appeerence, discerning locals know this to be the best place anywhere for noodle soups, especially *Talumein*, flavoured with egg drop, black mushroom and a choice of chicken, pork or beef. Open daily 9am–9pm.

Hotel Gahsel, opposite the offices of Royal Insurance Corporation of Bhutan,

as vegetarian food. If your stomach has become used to local food, try their south Indian rice pancake *uttapam*, and, *dosa*, crisp rice rolls with fillings of potato and seasonal vegetables. Daily 9am–10pm.

The plush **Blue Poppy**, (named after the national flower) is found in the same square as the Swiss Bakery and Hotel Taktsang. Serves mainly fine, upscale Bhutanese, Indian, Chinese and Continental dishes. Open daily 10 am–10pm.

Hotel Druk Yul, next to Hotel Taktsang and Swiss Bakery, offers a wide repertoire of Tibetan dishes, featuring exotica like marinated radish salads, sliced meats called *shaftra*, and steamed buns and dumplings. Open daily 7am–10pm.

Hotel Centrepoint's menu is unexceptional though reasonably priced. In addition, it is very conveniently located around the corner from the Bhutan National Bank, the Bhutan Postal Service and Thimphu Police Station. Open daily 10am–9pm, except on the last Sunday of the month.

The **Thimphu Golf Club Restaurant**, makes a great setting for a romantic dinner, overlooking the rolling greens of the capital's 9-hole golf course and picturesque Tashichhodzong and the SAARC Building beyond. At the far end of the valley, twinkling lights appear to reach skywards to join the star-filled night. Open daily 10am–10pm.

Nightlife

It is 11pm on Saturday. Except for the occasional howl of a stray dog, the streets of Thimphu have fallen silent, as usual. But somewhere at the end of Wogzin Lam, past Jomolhari Hotel, and the Druk Sherig Guest House, the pulsating beat of dance music beckons. The sounds are faint first, then stronger as you draw near.

Welcome to **Club X**, named, according to its owner – a young Bhutanese man known to senior UN diplomats, government officials and friends simply as Max – to honour the brevity of the syllable 'X'. But it seems more a nod to its clientele, who, with their interesting range of professional and educational backgrounds and their relative youth, could easily be described as Bhutan's Generation X. Housed in an abandoned warehouse at the end of a dark, narrow alley, the scene is oddly bohemian in this land of serene temples and Buddhist quiet.

The dance floor at Club X thrives on *bhangra*, an Indian fusion pop from the UK, but originally a dance form developed by the farmers of Punjab, and the standard fare of Billboard dance hits. Open Saturdays 8.30pm to the wee hours of the morning.

If the appearance of Club X and other weekend discotheques is an indication, young Bhutanese are learning to party, and will use any western holiday as excuse to organise dances. Besides the occasional Charity Ball attended by Thimphu's high society, April Fool's Day, St. Valentine's Day and, even, Halloween have been deemed as an appropriate party events. Christmas Eve, New Year's Eve and Losar, the Bhutanese New Year's Day, see the biggest, best attended parties at local discotheques. Although it would be silly to travel to Bhutan for its nightlife, it can be interesting to take a peek once you are here.

Located in a huge basement of Hotel Druk Yul, near Swiss Bakery, **The Hub** is the place to be on Friday nights. Deejays play a mix of reggae, rock and roll and Indian MTV music.

Also on Fridays, the **TGIF** (Thank God Its Friday) **Club** at Pinewood Hotel, atop a ridge overlooking the entrance to the valley, comes alive. Popular with international development workers, it offers a buffet dinner, dart games and, on occasion, rounds of Bingo for the truly bored.

At the **Hotel Riverview's** discotheque, young and energetic music is favoured, including rave, pop and hip-hop. Open on select holidays and weekends.

Calendar of Special Events

Bhutan's religious festivals mainly take place during the spring and autumn months, the dates of which are fixed according to the Bhutanese lunar calendar. Celebrations may range from complex rituals to the protective deities to simple recitation or chanting of prayers and offerings to the ubi-quitous mountain gods.

The best known and most elaborate of the festivals is the *tshechu*, held in honour of Guru Rinpoche and commemorating his great deeds. *Tshechu* means Tenth Day, when the good deeds of Guru Rinpoche are believed to have taken place though, in practice, not all *tshechu* fall on the tenth day of the month.

Chaams or religious dances are performed at *tshechu* to teach the precepts of Buddhism, to subdue evil spirits or celebrate the greatness of Buddha. Performed by monks or laymen, depending on the occasion, the dancers wear extravagant costumes and carved masks. The performers are usually accomplished athletes as well because some of the dances last over an hour and involve much leaping and rotating.

A holy celebration is not complete without *atsaras*, clowns who wear expressive masks, make ribald jokes and mock the dancers to get the public roaring with laughter.

An important *tshechu* might include the display of a large appliqued *thangka,* called a *thongdrol*, which usually represents Guru Rinpoche and his Eight Manifestations.

Festivals for the Bhutanese

Black Demon or De Nakchung

are a combination of both the spiritual and the social. Apart from dances and rituals as a vehicle to impart Buddhist teachings, there is also the chance to meet family, friends and acquaintances, to show off new clothes and jewellery and perhaps forget the hard grind of daily chores. For visitors, it's a chance to watch the colouful spectacle of Bhutanese dancing, praying, eating and drinking in a uniquely convivial atmosphere where humour and devotion mix astonishingly well. Participating in a festival is one of the best ways to appreciate the essence of the Bhutanese character.

Famous Dances

The most popular *chaam* is the **Black Hat** dance, where dancers wear large hats, high boots and silk brocade costumes. This dance relates the 8th-century murder of the anti-Buddhist Tibetan king, Langdarma, by a Tantric priest. Other interesting dances include the **Drummers From Dametsi**,

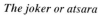

The joker or atsara

composed by Pemalingpa in the 16th century after he had a vision of the paradise of Guru Rinpoche; the **Hunter and the Deer**, depicting the conversion of a hunter to Buddhism by Milarepa, the 12th-century saint and poet; **Judgement of the Dead**, which relates what happens to those who commit evil deeds; the **Noblemen and the Ladies**, a ribald play about the greatness of forgiving; the dance of the **Guardians of the Cremation Grounds**, featuring skeletons and other ghoulish props; the dance of the **Eight Manifestations of Guru Rinpoche**, marking the end of the *tshechu* and culminating in a general blessing for the public; and **Pachham, Dance of the Heroes**, performed all over Bhutan by young monks wearing crowns, resplendent brocade jackets and swirling silks.

While there are *chaams* where dancers perform their own music, the more religiously significant dances are supported by cast of musicians from the clergy, clashing hand-held cymbals and blowing long horns while chanting from holy texts. Apart from maintaining the tempo of the dances, the words and music of the monastic ensemble make the ceremonies more spiritually potent.

Festival Dates

The Bhutanese year starts in February/March and has 12 months of 30 days each. Festivals set by this lunar calendar have dates that vary each year. The government publishes a list of festival dates and this is usually sent out to travel agants.

February–March

Losar, the Bhutanese New Year festival is a two-day government holiday. Essentially a private family affair, it is also celebrated with archery contests.

Punakha Serda is a one-day religious holiday commemorating the 17th-century victory of the Bhutanese over the Tibetans.

March–April

Paro Tshechu is a 5-day religious festival celebrated only in Paro. The famous giant *thangka* featuring Guru Rinpoche is shown at dawn on the last day, and people throng to get blessings on this extra special day

April–May

Shabdrung Kuchoe is a national holiday commemmorating the death anniversary of the Shabdrung Ngawang Namgyel who

Judgement of the Dead dance

was responsible for unifying Bhutan in the 17th century.

June–July

2 June: His Majesty King Jigme Singye Wangchuck's coronation anniversary is a national holiday with parades marching past the district headquarters.

26 July: National holiday commemmorating the death anniversary of the third King Jigme Dorje Wangchuck.

September–November

Blessed Rainy Day is a one-day religious national holiday.

Thimphu Dromchoe and **Tshechu** are two religious festivals that follow each other. Celebrated only in Thimphu with one day for Dromchoe and three days for the *tshechu*.

Wangdiphodrang Tshechu is a 3-day religious holiday only in Wangdiphodrang.

Dasain and **Diwali** are Hindu religious festivals celebrated by the southern Bhutanese.

11 November: His Majesty King Jigme Singye Wangchuck's birthday is a 3-day national holiday marked throughout the Kingdom with parades.

December–January

Tongsa Tshechu is a 4-day religious festival celebrated only in Tongsa.

17 December: National Day commemorates the **coronation** of the first King Ugyen Wangchuck at Punakha in 1907.

Chaam in Thimphu

Practical Information

By Air

Entry is easiest by air. Druk Air is the national airline, sometimes known as Royal Bhutan Airlines, and the only airline that flies into Bhutan. It operates two BAe 146 4-engine jets carrying 77 passengers twice a week from Delhi and Kathmandu, once a week from Calcutta and Dhaka and twice a week from Bangkok.

Schedules and rates may change at short notice so check with the Druk Air agent in the country of departure. Airfares are relatively costly and payable in foreign exchange with no excursion or concession rates. Druk Air's in-flight service is good, with a friendly crew, colourful handwoven blankets to keep warm and French wine served on board.

Thai International offices in major cities in the US and Europe can issue your Druk-Air ticket, but only *after* you have confirmed your booking through the Druk-Air offices in Thimphu, Kathmandu, Delhi, Dhaka, Calcutta or Bangkok. Druk-Air requires proof of visa clearance from Thimphu before issuing a ticket (see pg 81).

From October to early April, the flight to Bhutan is especially spectacular with the whole of the eastern Himalaya visible, including famous giants such as Everest, Kangchenjunga and Jomolhari.

Bhutan's only airport is in Paro and is an hour's drive from the capital, Thimphu. A tourist bus or the Druk Air coach will take you from Paro to Thimphu. Paro airport is located in the mountains at 2,200m (7,220 ft) and the weather can sometimes cause delays, especially during the summer monsoon. When leaving Bhutan, avoid tight connecting schedules for ongoing flights.

Following recent renovations, the airport has central heating – a blessing in the bitter cold of Paro winter mornings – a restaurant, bookshop, accessibility lifts for the disabled, and television monitors displaying flight information.

By Road

Travelling overland is not recommended unless you are with a group or are particularly adventurous. Phuntsholing is the entry point on the Indian border in the state of West Bengal, a 5-hour drive from Darjeeling or a 3-hour drive from the nearest Indian airport of Bagdogra. The latter is linked by daily Indian Airlines flights from Delhi or Calcutta. The nearest train station is Siliguri or New Jalpaiguri.

Your Bhutanese tour operator will receive you in Phuntsholing. After an overnight stop, it is a further 6 hours by road to Thimphu or Paro.

TRAVEL ESSENTIALS

Visas and Passports

Independent travellers are not granted entry into Bhutan unless invited by the government or if working for an accredited aid agency. Indian and other South Asian Association for Regional Cooperation (SAARC) country nationals are not bound by these rules.

Valid passports and visas are essential. There is a fixed government quota on the number of tourists allowed entry into Bhutan, most of which is taken up by travel agents. Tourist operations are handled by private Bhutanese companies but prices are fixed by the government tourist board. Flat rates, one for cultural tours and the other for treks, include transportation, guides, accommodations and food, and do not vary with the seasons.

The best option is to join a group with an international tour operator who will handle all the arrangements and formalities. Tour operators are listed on page 90–91.

Visas are not issued abroad but are stamped in your passport upon arrival in Paro and cost US$20. However, the process is not as easy as it sounds: your Druk Air ticket cannot be issued until Druk Air receives visa clearance from Thimphu. To apply for a visa, contact either your host agency or foreign or Bhutanese tour operator. State your departing airport for Bhutan, or Phuntsholing if you come by land, and give all your passport details at least 15 days before the date of arrival. When it is processed, your visa clearance will be sent to the Druk Air office of your departing airport for Bhutan, or directly to Phuntsholing.

You need a permit to travel in Bhutan outside of Paro and Thimphu. If you are not part of a tour group, you should know that the permit takes at least two days to obtain from Thimphu's Immigration Office so do not plan to leave Thimphu immediately and do check official holidays. You need two passport-size photos and the complete list of all the places you wish to visit. In addition, a second permit is required if you wish to

visit restricted monasteries and dzongs in Bhutan. This can be obtained from the Special Commission for Cultural Affairs in Thimphu, but be forewarned that this permit is difficult to obtain if you are not a Buddhist.

Vaccinations

Although no compulsory vaccinations are required to enter Bhutan, recommended are typhoid, tetanus, poliomyelitis jabs and a shot of gamma-globulin which protects against hepatitis A. Complete vaccination coverage would include hepatitis B, rabies and meningitis but is unnecessary for a short stay.

Customs

Customs laws forbid the export of antiques or religious objects. Paro airport customs officers are very efficient in this regard.

Always ask for a receipt with your purchases as unrecorded items may be confiscated by the customs officers. Have any new religious objects, such as prayer wheels and *thangka*s that you have bought or been given cleared by the Antiquities Department in Thimphu. Items purchased from Thimphu's Government Handicrafts Emporium are exempted from this requirement. If you are carrying religious items from another country, declare them on your customs form upon arrival in Bhutan to avoid any problems when departing.

It is forbidden to export samples of butterflies, plants or flowers.

Weather

The temperature and weather can change quickly and you may experience different climates in one day. Depending on the altitude, you may be freezing on top of a pass and two hours later be in semi-tropical jungle. It is difficult to accurately generalise about the climate of Bhutan because of the variations in elevations and seasons. The southern belt has a similar climate to West Bengal – cool and sunny in winter and hot and rainy in summer. The central valleys share the same pleasant climate but the eastern ones are lower and warmer. Winter from November to March is generally sunny except for the occasional snowfall; temperatures can be relatively warm during the day (16°C/61°F) but fall below freezing at night. Spring, from mid-March to May, is cool and often stormy as it slowly warms up. The monsoon can start as early as mid-June and last until end

Religious items must be declared

September. These months are warm and cloudy with showers falling mostly in the evening and at night. October is a gorgeous autumn month with clear skies, warm days and cool nights.

Clothing

Practical and comfortable clothes are appropriate, with dressy outfits only necessary if you are in Bhutan on business. Because of the variety of climates you may encounter in one day, choose garments which can be layered, and peeled off as required depending on the temperature changes. From June to September cottons and a good woollen sweater should be enough, whilst from October to May you must also bring a down jacket or a warm coat. Do not underestimate the cold, especially in winter when offices and hotels are usually poorly heated. Hot water bottles are available in the hotels. A raincoat is not really necessary; it is better to bring an umbrella.

A pair of loafers or sneakers are the only footwear required unless you are trekking. Do not expect to buy shoes in Thimphu except thongs and it is often difficult for Westerners to find their sizes.

Always dress conservatively. Shorts, mini-skirts and halter tops, besides being unsuitable for the climate, are definite no-nos as the local population is not used to the display of bare skin.

Electricity

Officially 220 volts but the power supply can be erratic or non-existent depending on where you are. Be careful as the power sometimes fluctuates from 150 volts to 300 volts causing irreparable damage to sophisticated equipment.

Indian-made batteries are available almost everywhere but their quality is quite poor. Bring your own supply of alkaline batteries.

Time Difference

Bhutan is 6 hours ahead of GMT and 30 minutes ahead of India.

MONEY MATTERS

Currency

The currency is the Ngultrum, divided into Chetrums, and is at par with the Indian Rupee. The Indian Rupee is also legal tender in Bhutan. US$1 at time of press was equivalent to 34 Ngultrums. Travellers cheques in US and Canadian dollars, Japanese yen, German mark, French and Swiss francs and British sterling can be changed at the bank in Thimphu and major hotels. In smaller towns, US dollar travellers cheques and cash are the most widely accepted currency.

Credit Cards

Personal cheques are not accepted and credit cards are still a rarity. Only a few restaurants and shopping outlets in Thimphu accept the American Express card. Others such as Visa and Mastercard have yet to be introduced.

Tipping and Gifts

Small gifts are important in Bhutanese custom, probably more so than most other places in the world. Posters, keychains, stickers and other such souvenirs from your country are welcome and more appropriate than monetary tips.

Taxes

A departure tax of 300 Ngultrum (US$9) is levied at Paro airport.

GETTING AROUND

Taxi

Taxis are unreliable and expensive. Use them only in emergencies.

Bus

Local buses are not very frequent but they are cheap. However you cannot be in a hurry and must be prepared for some adventure and discomfort, especially when the bus turns out to be a truck and you have to cross a 4,000-m (13,000-ft) pass in winter.

Car

If alone and want to see as much as possible in a short time, you should hire a car. If you are with a group, the tour operator will provide the vehicles.

Renting a car is not expensive by Western standards. The rates are government-controlled and are charged on a per kilometre basis after the daily lump sum that covers the first 50km (30 miles). A driver and petrol are included in the price. A 4-wheel drive vehicle is more expensive than a sedan and is essential for central and east Bhutan. When you rent a car, don't forget to note down the mileage in the morning and evening to avoid any disputes.

For more information, contact a travel agent in Thimphu.

HOURS AND HOLIDAYS

Business Hours

Government office hours are Monday to Friday 9am to 4pm in winter (November to March) and 9am to 5pm in summer (April to October). Banking hours are 9am to 1pm Monday to Friday, and 9 to 11am on Saturday. Most shops stay open until 8–9pm but all shops are closed on Tuesdays, except Thimphu's Handicraft Emporium.

ACCOMMODATION

Hotels and guesthouses cannot be booked by individuals from outside Bhutan so use this list only as a reference. Your tour operator or host will make the booking, though you can state your preference for a specific hotel. When not part of a package, a double room in the most expensive hotels should cost no more than US$30 a night.

Bumthang (Jakar)

SWISS GUESTHOUSE
Bumthang, Bhutan
Tel: 03-21126
A convivial atmosphere reminiscent of an alpine lodge. The food is good and the six rooms are clean and well-kept. The common bathroom is in the garden.

TAMSHING LODGE
Bumthang, Bhutan
Located on the way to Tamshing Monastery. Quiet setting and comfortable rooms.

WANGDUCHOELING HOTEL
Bumthang, Bhutan
Tel: 03-31107
Traditional style hotel in a lovely setting. All the rooms have attached bathrooms and wood stoves during winter.

Mongar

SHONGAR LODGE
Mongar, Bhutan
Tel: 04-41107
Close to the dzong, in a nice garden setting with views. The simple rooms have attached bathrooms.

THE DRUK KUENDEN
Mongar, Bhutan
Tel: 04-41107
Located in town, has basic but comfortable rooms. Order food in advance as it takes a long time to prepare.

Paro

DRUK HOTEL
Paro, Bhutan
Tel: 71-386
Grand hotel built in the style of a dzong with a stunning view of the valley, especially from the front suites with their floor-to-ceiling windows. Good dining room and lovely landscaped grounds.

GANGTEY RESORT
Paro, Bhutan
Tel: 71-113
Converted from a former mansion, this is the cheapest of the four hotels. Comfortable rooms with wonderful character.

KYICHU RESORT
Paro, Bhutan
Tel: 71-468
A Japanese-inspired hotel with comfortable cottages and beautiful garden. Located on the way to Drugyel Dzong.

OLATHANG
Paro, Bhutan
Tel: 71-453
Paro's oldest hotel, built in traditional style to house guests during the coronation of the fourth king. Restful ambience, with private cottages facing the valley and large grounds set amidst a flourishing pine forest.

Phuntsholing

DRUK HOTEL
Phuntsholing, Bhutan
Tel: 05-2428
The best hotel in town and conveniently located near the bus station. All rooms are airconditioned with attached bathrooms. The restaurant serves Continental, Chinese and Indian dishes.

KUENGA HOTEL
Phuntsholing, Bhutan
Tel: 05-2293

Avoid travelling during the monsoon

Just opposite the Druk Hotel. Basic and inexpensive. Rooms have fans and cold water only but the food is good. Recommended only for experienced travellers.

NAMGYEL HOTEL
Phuntsholing, Bhutan
Tel: 05-2374
Right on the main square. Most of the rooms are airconditioned and standard Chinese and Indian fare is offered.

Tashigang

KELLING LODGE
Tashigang, Bhutan
Tel: 04-21145
Spectacular position in a garden overlooking the dzong. Rooms are simple but comfortable with attached bathrooms.

Thimpu

DRUK HOTEL
PO Box 176
Thimphu, Bhutan
Tel: 2-22966; Fax: 2-22677
Near the clock tower, very comfortable, with a good restaurant, health club and beauty parlour. Caters to Indian tourists and foreign consultants.

DRUK SHERIG GUESTHOUSE
PO Box 188
Thimphu, Bhutan
Tel: 2-23652; Fax: 2-23614

A family-owned establishment next to the Jomolhari. Popular with Bhutan regulars, the rooms are comfortable and Bhutanese food can be ordered.

HOTEL RIVERVIEW
PO Box 309
Thimphu, Bhutan
Tel: 2-23497; Fax: 2-23496
The 'Sheraton' of hotels in Thimphu, opposite Changlimithang Stadium. Offers panoramic views, conference halls, a fine restaurant, discotheque, and a spacious sundeck to watch morning rays splash towering Himalayan ridges.

JOMOLHARI HOTEL
PO Box 308
Thimphu, Bhutan
Tel: 2-22747; Fax: 2-24412
Situated close to the Druk Hotel. In the same price range, and attracts a similar clientele. Boasts a good restaurant.

MOTITHANG HOTEL
PO Box 120
Thimphu, Bhutan
Tel: 2-22435; Fax: 2-22479
Located quite far from the centre of town in the prosperous suburb of Motithang. Caters to both tourist groups as well as official foreign delegations.

TAKTSANG
PO Box 199
Thimphu, Bhutan
Tel: 2-22102; Fax: 2-23248
A new hotel conveniently located above the main traffic roundabout on Norzim Lam. Caters mainly to tourist groups.

Tongsa

SHERUBLING LODGE
Tongsa, Bhutan
Tel: 03-21116
Simple rooms with attached bathrooms. Bhutanese food is served buffet-style.

YANGKHYLL HOTEL
Tongsa, Bhutan
Tel: 03-21126
Located at the end of the main street. Basic but clean rooms with common bathrooms. Bhutanese and Tibetan dishes are

served in a convivial kitchen in this hotel popular with foreign residents.

Wangdiphodrang /Punakha

DECHEN COTTAGES
Mendegang, Bhutan
Owned by Thinphu's Dechen Hotel. Built in 1990 in traditional style and serves Bhutanese food. Located in a lovely setting above the Thimphu to Wangdiphodrang road in the Mendegang region.

DRAGON'S NEST RESORT
Wangdiphodrang, Bhutan
Tel: 81-367
This new hotel has 17 spacious rooms with balconies overlooking the jade-green waters of Puna Tsangchu river, luxurious European baths, hot water around the clock, a restaurant, and wonderful views of ancient Wangdiphodrang Dzong.

GANGTEY THANKA GUEST HOUSE
Wangdiphodrang, Bhutan
Tel: 81-250
Clean but basic rooms.

WANGDI KYICHU RESORT
Wangdiphodrang, Bhutan
Tel: 2-24963
At the confluence of two fast running streams, this upscale resort at Chuzomsa, Wangdiphodrang, has 21 rooms and one suite. An ideal place to break your journey or to rest after one of several hikes around the two valleys.

ZANGTO PELRI HOTEL
Punakha, Bhutan
Tel: 81-125
Plush, new hotel. No choice really as this is the only place to stay in Punakha.

HEALTH AND EMERGENCIES

Hygiene

Generally speaking, do not expect the same health and hygiene standards as in the West. If you are a hypochondriac or a cleanliness junkie, give Bhutan a miss.

Have a thorough check-up before you leave home, take all precautions and hope for the best. Amoeba, *giardia* and worms are all rife and it is recommended that you have a stool test when you go home. Avoid eating raw and unpeeled fruit or vegetables, ice cubes and water which has not been boiled or purified. Malaria is endemic at low altitudes and ordinary Chloroquin is not sufficient any more. If you have to stay below 1,300m (4,250ft), take Lariam instead.

Altitude sickness can be a problem during the first few days but the discomfort disappears rapidly if you do not exert yourself too much. Take some aspirin in case of headache and try to sleep as much as possible. Do not drink alcohol for the first two days and be sure to drink more fluids than usual to help your body acclimatise.

Pharmacies

Bring your own medicines as far as possible, plus some disposable syringes, a thermometer, sleeping-pills (altitude can hinder sleep), anti-nausea pills, anti-diarrhoea pills, water purifying tablets, oral rehydration packets, eye drops, antibiotic ointment and anti-histamine ointment. Pharmacies in Thimphu stock antibiotics, but prescriptions are necessary.

Medical Services

Thimphu, Tashigang and Bumthang hospitals are staffed with competent doctors and offer basic services but there are no intensive care units.

COMMUNICATIONS AND NEWS
Post

Mail service within the country and airmail abroad is generally reliable, but can be slow or erratic at times. Bhutanese stamps are prized collector's items. Visit the Philatelic Bureau at the Thimphu post office and ask for first day cover envelopes and albums. If the post office is closed, you can also find stamps at Thimphu's Ethometho shop and at the postal counter in the Druk Shopping Complex.

Telephone

In 1990–91 direct satellite telephone links and fax machines were introduced. It is now possible to direct dial to and from Thimphu and most other places in Bhutan internationally. The Bhutan country code is 975 and area codes are as follows: Thimphu (2); Paro (71); Tongsa and Bumthang (03); Mongar, Tashigang and Samdrup Jongkhar (04); Phuntsholing (5); Punakha (841) and Wangdiphodrang (81).

Telecommunications within the country have improved, and you can now call and sometimes fax most district headquarters. For remote areas, wireless transmissions are still necessary.

Media

There is no television in Bhutan but many people in Thimphu own video recorders, and video cassettes are widely available.

The BBS, Bhutan Broadcasting Service, broadcasts in Dzongkha, English and Nepali from Monday to Saturday 5–9pm on 60 mb 5025 KHz and FM 96 in Thimphu; and on Sundays from 10am–4pm on 49 mb 6035 KHz and FM 96. The English news is at 8.15pm Monday to Saturday and at 3pm on Sunday.

With a shortwave radio it is easy to tune into BBC and VoA.

There is only one newspaper, the Kuensel, which is published every Saturday in English, Dzongkha and Nepali. International weeklies and some Indian dailies are available at the bookshops in Thimphu.

USEFUL INFORMATION
Bookshops and Maps

In Thimphu, Pekhang, next to the cinema hall, carries the best selection of maps, books on Bhutan, Buddhism and the region, and also novels. DSB Books, across from the clocktower, also has novels and good books on Tibetan Buddhism and Bhutan.

Photography

There are several photo shops in Thimphu but they do not sell equipment or accessories and the quality of their prints is not of international standards. You may find colour print film but slides are more difficult. You are advised to bring everything you need including batteries for your camera and an ample stock of film.

Cigarettes

Indian and some foreign cigarette brands are available in Thimphu but not outside the capital as there is a tendency to ban smoking. Bring with you what you need.

Laundry

It is usually possible to have clothes washed and ironed in one day. Dry cleaning is impossible except in Thimphu and Phuntsholing and will take at least a week. If you want to wash delicate clothes yourself, buy liquid Ezee, which is least abrasive of the locally available washing compounds.

Tour Checklist

The following items are useful on a short tour:

- practical clothing including a warm jacket
- flashlight with spare batteries
- sturdy sneakers
- Swiss pocket knife
- water bottle
- hat or scarf
- sunglasses
- foldable umbrella
- extra passport size photos for permits etc.
- lip balm and moisturising cream
- protective sunscreen
- personal toiletries and medicine
- shaving kit and extra blades (more practical than an electric shaver)
- Binoculars, a shortwave radio, and a Walkman.

Trekking Checklist

If you are trekking, you will need the following items:

- day pack to carry essentials for a day's walk
- good sleeping bag
- small inflatable pillow
- head torch (very handy to keep your hands free in a tent)
- poncho
- towel
- flea powder and anti-lice shampoo
- walking shoes
- small mirror
- several plastic sacks to pack your personal belongings inside your bags (as protection against the rain)
- plastic mug and spoon
- pack of wet tissues
- toilet paper

LANGUAGE

Dzongkha, the language of the western region, is the national language. English is the medium of instruction and is spoken by government officials and businessmen. The Nepali language is commonly used in the south, Bumthangkha and Khengkha is spoken in the centre, and Sharchopkha in the east.

In the past most Bhutanese names and words were spelt haphazardly and in different ways, for instance: *Dorji, Dorjee, Dorje,* or *Penjo, Penjore, Penjor.* The standard, if any, was set by the most common use of the word. Since 1990, efforts at formally establishing roman representations of the 30 consonants and four vowels in Dzongkha has resulted in some measure of standardisation for street and place names, and for names of the country's 20 districts. However, old spellings still surface in both official literature and public signboards. But, there is no need to despair as the old and the new spellings do not vary too greatly.

New Official Spellings

Old	New
Tashigang	*Trashigang*
Tongsa	Trongsa
Wangdiphodrang	Wangue**phodrang**
Phuntsholing	Phuentsholing
Kuje	Kurjey

Unusual Bhutanese stamps

Lhuentse	Lhuntse
Chukha	Chhukha
Simtokha	Semtokha

Glossary of Useful Terms

arak – distilled alcohol made from cereals or maize

Ashi – Princess, lady of royal blood

Aum – form of address Madam, Mrs

banchung – small round double bamboo basket

Brokpas (or bjops) – yak-herders living at high altitudes

bura – Bhutanese rough raw silk

chaam – religious dances

chhang – fermented alcohol made from cereals

Chenrezi – Bodhisattva of Compassion, Avalokiteshwara in Sanskrit

choeke – classical language, written Tibetan

chorten – stupa, Buddhist monument

chu – water, river

Dasho – Sir, honorary title conferred by the kind, also a male person of royal blood

Desi – Temporal Rulers of Bhutan between 1650 and 1907

doma – betel leaves, areca nut and lime

dratshang – state monastic community

Drukpa – followers of the religious school of the Drukpa Kagyudpa, the official religious school of Bhutan

drukpa – citizens of Bhutan, Bhutanese

Druk Yul – literally 'Land of the Dragon', name of Bhutan in Bhutanese

duar – refers to the 18 accesses to the Indian plains

dzong – fortress; in Bhutan refers to the fortress which houses the administration and the district monastic community

Dzongdag – 'Lord of the Dzong', District Commissioner

dzongkha – language of west Bhutan, now the national language

dzongkhag – district (there are 20 districts in Bhutan)

emadatsi – national dish of Bhutan; a curry of chillies in cheese sauce

gelong – fully ordained monk

go – male dress, similar to a kimono

gomchen – religious lay person acting as village priest, mostly in central and east Bhutan

gompa (gonpa) – monastery

Guru Rinpoche – saint who in the 8th century introduced Tantric Buddhism in Bhutan. Founder of the Nyingmapa religious school

Je Khenpo – spiritual head of the Drukpa Kagyudpa religious school in Bhutan

kabne – ceremonial scarf worn by men on official occasions and in religious places

kata – ceremonial white scarf which is offered as an auspicious gesture

kadrinche – thank you

kera – belt

kira – female traditional dress

koma – silver brooches for women

kuzuzangpo – hello, how are you?

la – pass

la, lasso la – yes, in polite form

lam – street

lama – religious practitioner

lha – god

lhakhang – temple

Lopon – master

Lyonpo – minister

Ngalong – inhabitants of western Bhutan

Nyingmapa – follower of the Nyingma religious school

onju – female blouse

Pemalingpa (1450–1521) – a saint who had contributed greatly to the spread of the Nyingma religious school in central and east Bhutan

Penlop – title, governors of Tongsa, Paro

and Daga dzongs from the 17th century to the mid-20th century

Shabdrung Ngawang Namgyel (1594–1651) – great lama of the Drukpa Kagyudpa religious school who unified Bhutan in the mid-17th century under the hegemony of this school and gave the country its administrative system

Sharchopas – inhabitants of east Bhutan

tertoen – religious treasure finder

thangka – religious painting on cloth

thongdrol – huge thangka believed to 'liberate by sight'

toego – female jacket or male blouse

Tshechu – religious festival in honour of Guru Rinpoche

tsho – lake

tsongkhang – shop

utse – central tower in a dzong

yatra – twill-wool colourful fabric from Bumthang

zampa – bridge

USEFUL ADDRESSES

Airline Office

DRUK AIR
Thimphu, Bhutan
Tel: 2-22215; Fax: 2-22775

Local Government Offices

TOURISM AUTHORITY OF BHUTAN
PO Box 126
Thimphu, Bhutan
Tel: 2-23251; Fax: 2-23695

IMMIGRATION OFFICE
Ministry of Home Affairs
Tashichho Dzong
Thimphu, Bhutan
Tel: 2-23127

SPECIAL COMMISSION FOR
CULTURAL AFFAIRS
Thimphu, Bhutan
Tel: 2-22694

PROTOCOL OFFICE
Ministry of Foreign Affairs
SAARC Convention Centre
Thimphu, Bhutan
Tel: 2-22118

Overseas Embassies/Offices

THE ROYAL BHUTANESE EMBASSY
Chandragupta Marg
Chanakyapuri
New Delhi 10021, India
Tel: 11-609218; Fax: 11-6187 6710

THE ROYAL BHUTANESE EMBASSY
House No 58, Road No 3A
Dhanmondi R.A.
Dhaka, Bangladesh
Tel: 2-505418

THE PERMANENT BHUTANESE MISSION
TO THE UN IN NEW YORK
2 UN Plaza (27th floor)
New York, New York 10017, USA
Tel: 212 8261919; Fax: 212-8262998

THE PERMANENT BHUTANESE MISSION
TO THE UN IN GENEVA
Palais des Nations
17-19 Champ d'Anier
CH-1209 Geneva, Switzerland
Tel: 022 -7987971; Fax: 022-7882593

LES AMIS DU BHOUTAN
(ASSOCIATION, LOI 1901)
20 rue du Maine
75014 Paris, France
Tel: 1-43351723

Travel Agencies

India

MALBROS TRAVELS
403 Nirmal Towers
Barakhamba Road
New Delhi 100001, India
Tel: 11-3322859; Telex: 31-61773

Nepal

SHAMBALA TRAVELS
P.O. Box 4794, Durbar Marg
Kathmandu, Nepal
Tel: 1-225166; Fax: 1-227229
Telex: 2627

United States

BHUTAN TRAVEL SERVICE
120 East 56th Street, Suite 1430
New York, New York 10022, USA
Tel: 212 8386382; Fax: 212 7501269
Telex: 220896

INNER ASIA
2627 Lombard Street
San Francisco
California 94123, USA
Tel: 415 9220448; Fax: 415 3465535
Telex: 278716

GULLIVER'S TRAVEL
755 Santa Rosa Street
San Luis Obispo
California 93401, USA
Tel: 805-5414141; Fax: 805-5414832

Japan

SAIYU TRAVEL
Shinsekai Building 5F,
2-2-Jimbocho, Kanda, Chiyoda-ku
Tokyo, Japan
Tel: 3-2371391; Fax: 3-2371396
Telex: 2323189

France

ASSINTER
38 rue Madame
75006 Paris, France
Tel: 1-45444587; Fax:1-45441809

Bhutan

CHUNDU TRAVELS
Norzim Lam, Thimphu, Bhutan
Tel: 2-22592; Fax: 2-22645

ETHOMETHO (Ms Dago Beda)
Thimphu, Bhutan
Tel: 2-23693; Fax: 2-22884

TAKIN TRAVEL
P O Box 454, Thimphu, Bhutan
Tel: 2-23129; Fax: 2-23130

TASHI TOURS
P O Box 423, Thimphu, Bhutan
Tel: 2-23361; Fax; 2-23666

YANGPHEL TRAVELS
(Mr Ugyen Rinzing)
Gatoen Lam, Thimphu, Bhutan
Tel: 2-23293; Fax: 2-22897

YUDRUK TOURS
(Ms Sonam Wangmo)
Thimphu, Bhutan
Tel: 2-23461; Fax: 2-22116

FURTHER READING

Adams, Barbara S. *Traditional Bhutanese Textiles*, Bangkok, 1984

Aris, Michael. *Bhutan: The Early History of a Himalayan Kingdom*, Warminster, 1979

Aris, Michael. *The Raven Crown: the Origins of the Buddhist Monarchy in Bhutan*, London, 1994

Bartholomew, Mark. *Thunder Dragon Textiles From Bhutan*, Tokyo, 1985

Barker, David K. *Designs of Bhutan*, Bangkok, 1985

Berry, Steven K. *The Thunder Dragon Kingdom: A Mountaineering Expedition to Bhutan*, Malborough, Seattle 1988

Choden, Kunzang. *Bhutanese Tales of the Yeti*, Bangkok, 1997

Choden, Kunzang. *Folktales of Bhutan*, Bangkok 1993

Department of Works, Housing and Roads. *An Introduction to the Architecture of Bhutan*, Thimphu, 1993

Dago Tshering (ed). *Bhutan: Himalayan Kingdom*, Royal Government of the Kingdom of Bhutan, 1979

Edmunds, Tom Owen. *Bhutan: Land of the Thunder Dragon*, London 1988

Imaeda, Yoshiro and J.O.C.V. *Manual of Spoken Dzongkha*, Thimpu 1990

Insight Guide: South Asia. Apa Publications, 1994.

Inskipp, Carol and Tim. *An Introduction to Birdwatching in Bhutan*, Thimphu, 1995

Myers, Diana K. and Bean, Susan S. *From the Land of the Thunder Dragon: Textile Arts of Bhutan*, London, 1994

Nishioka Keiji and Nakao Sasuke. *Flowers of Bhutan*, Tokyo 1984

Rose, Leo E. *The Politics of Bhutan*, New York 1977

Stapleton, Chris. *Bamboos of Bhutan*, London 1994

Solverson, Howard. *The Jesuit and the Dragon*, Outremont, 1995

Tsewang Padma; Tashi, Phuntshok (Khenpo); Butters, Chris; Saetereng Sigmund. *The Treasure Revealer of Bhutan: Pema Lingpa, the Terma Tradition and its Critics*, Kathmandu, 1995

Ura, Karma. *The Hero with a Thousand Eyes*, Thimphu, 1995

Index

ACKNOWLEDGMENTS

Photography	**Francoise Pommaret** *and*
39	**Belinda Edwards**
35, 37, 42B, 49, 87	**Chimme Dorji**
50	**Diane Summers**
13B, 53	**Eric Valli**
42/43T	**Mingma Norbu Sherpa**
29, 40T, 44, 47, 75B, 87	**Wendy Lama**
Update Editor	**Karma Singye**
Handwriting	**V. Barl**
Cover Design	**Patrick Wong**
Maps	**Berndtson & Berndtson**

Insight Guides

Alaska
Alsace
Amazon Wildlife
American Southwest
Amsterdam
Argentina
Atlanta
Athens
Australia
Austria
Bahamas
Bali
Baltic States
Bangkok
Barbados
Barcelona
Bay of Naples
Beijing
Belgium
Belize
Berlin
Bermuda
Boston
Brazil
Brittany
Brussels
Budapest
Buenos Aires
Burgundy
Burma (Myanmar)
Cairo
Calcutta
California
Canada
Caribbean
Catalonia
Channel Islands
Chicago
Chile
China
Cologne
Continental Europe
Corsica
Costa Rica
Crete
Crossing America
Cuba
Cyprus
Czech & Slovak
  Republics
Delhi, Jaipur, Agra
Denmark

Dresden
Dublin
Düsseldorf
East African Wildlife
East Asia
Eastern Europe
Ecuador
Edinburgh
Egypt
Finland
Florence
Florida
France
Frankfurt
French Riviera
Gambia & Senegal
Germany
Glasgow
Gran Canaria
Great Barrier Reef
Great Britain
Greece
Greek Islands
Hamburg
Hawaii
Hong Kong
Hungary
Iceland
India
India's Western
  Himalaya
Indian Wildlife
Indonesia
Ireland
Israel
Istanbul
Italy
Jamaica
Japan
Java
Jerusalem
Jordan
Kathmandu
Kenya
Korea
Lisbon
Loire Valley
London
Los Angeles
Madeira
Madrid
Malaysia
Mallorca & Ibiza
Malta

Marine Life in the
  South China Sea
Melbourne
Mexico
Mexico City
Miami
Montreal
Morocco
Moscow
Munich
Namibia
Native America
Nepal
Netherlands
New England
New Orleans
New York City
New York State
New Zealand
Nile
Normandy
Northern California
Northern Spain
Norway
Oman & the UAE
Oxford
Old South
Pacific Northwest
Pakistan
Paris
Peru
Philadelphia
Philippines
Poland
Portugal
Prague
Provence
Puerto Rico
Rajasthan
Rhine
Rio de Janeiro
Rockies
Rome
Russia
St Petersburg
San Francisco
Sardinia
Scotland
Seattle
Sicily
Singapore
South Africa
South America
South Asia

South India
South Tyrol
Southeast Asia
Southeast Asia Wildlife
Southern California
Southern Spain
Spain
Sri Lanka
Sweden
Switzerland
Sydney
Taiwan
Tenerife
Texas
Thailand
Tokyo
Trinidad & Tobago
Tunisia
Turkey
Turkish Coast
Tuscany
Umbria
US National Parks East
US National Parks West
Vancouver
Venezuela
Venice
Vienna
Vietnam
Wales
Washington DC
Waterways of Europe
Wild West
Yemen

Insight Pocket Guides

Aegean Islands ★
Algarve ★
Alsace
Amsterdam ★
Athens ★
Atlanta ★
Bahamas ★
Baja Peninsula ★
Bali ★
Bali *Bird Walks*
Bangkok ★
Barbados ★
Barcelona ★
Bavaria ★
Beijing ★
Berlin ★
Bermuda ★

nsight Guides

ver every major destination in every continent.

Bhutan★
Boston★
British Columbia★
Brittany★
Brussels★
Budapest &
 Surroundings★
Canton★
Chiang Mai★
Chicago★
Corsica★
Costa Blanca★
Costa Brava★
Costa del
Sol/Marbella★
Costa Rica★
Crete★
Denmark★
Fiji★
Florence★
Florida★
Florida Keys★
French Riviera★
Gran Canaria★
Hawaii★
Hong Kong★
Hungary
Ibiza★
Ireland★
Ireland's Southwest★
Israel★
Istanbul★
Jakarta★
Jamaica★
Kathmandu *Bikes &*
 Hikes★
Kenya★
Kuala Lumpur★
Lisbon★
Loire Valley★
London★
Macau
Madrid★
Malacca
Maldives
Mallorca★
Malta★
Mexico City★
Miami★
Milan★
Montreal★
Morocco★
Moscow
Munich★

Nepal★
New Delhi
New Orleans★
New York City★
New Zealand★
Northern California★
Oslo/Bergen★
Paris★
Penang★
Phuket★
Prague★
Provence★
Puerto Rico★
Quebec★
Rhodes★
Rome★
Sabah★
St Petersburg★
San Francisco★
Sardinia
Scotland★
Seville★
Seychelles★
Sicily★
Sikkim
Singapore★
Southeast England
Southern California★
Southern Spain★
Sri Lanka★
Sydney★
Tenerife★
Thailand★
Tibet★
Toronto★
Tunisia★
Turkish Coast★
Tuscany★
Venice★
Vienna★
Vietnam★
Yogyakarta
Yucatan Peninsula★

**★ = *Insight Pocket
Guides*
with Pull out Maps**

Insight Compact Guides

Algarve
Amsterdam
Bahamas
Bali
Bangkok

Barbados
Barcelona
Beijing
Belgium
Berlin
Brittany
Brussels
Budapest
Burgundy
Copenhagen
Costa Brava
Costa Rica
Crete
Cyprus
Czech Republic
Denmark
Dominican Republic
Dublin
Egypt
Finland
Florence
Gran Canaria
Greece
Holland
Hong Kong
Ireland
Israel
Italian Lakes
Italian Riviera
Jamaica
Jerusalem
Lisbon
Madeira
Mallorca
Malta
Milan
Moscow
Munich
Normandy
Norway
Paris
Poland
Portugal
Prague
Provence
Rhodes
Rome
St Petersburg
Salzburg
Singapore
Switzerland
Sydney
Tenerife
Thailand

Turkey
Turkish Coast
Tuscany
UK regional titles:
 Bath & Surroundings
 Cambridge & East
  Anglia
 Cornwall
 Cotswolds
 Devon & Exmoor
 Edinburgh
 Lake District
 London
 New Forest
 North York Moors
 Northumbria
 Oxford
 Peak District
 Scotland
 Scottish Highlands
 Shakespeare Country
 Snowdonia
 South Downs
 York
 Yorkshire Dales
USA regional titles:
 Boston
 Cape Cod
 Chicago
 Florida
 Florida Keys
 Hawaii: Maui
 Hawaii: Oahu
 Las Vegas
 Los Angeles
 Martha's Vineyard &
  Nantucket
 New York
 San Francisco
 Washington D.C.
Venice
Vienna
West of Ireland

NOTES